FIELD G

G000024371

PCs

PUBLISHED BY

Microsoft Press
A Division of Microsoft Corporation
One Microsoft Way
Redmond, Washington 98052-6399

Library of Congress Cataloging-in-Publication Data
Nelson, Stephen L., 1959-
  Field guide to PCs /Stephen L. Nelson.
     p.   cm.
  Includes index.
  ISBN 1-55615-842-4
  1. Microcomputers. I. Title.
QA76.5.N386   1995
004.165--dc20   95-25003
                                      CIP

Printed and bound in the United States of America.

1 2 3 4 5 6 7 8 9 QBP 9 8 7 6 5

Distributed to the book trade in Canada by Macmillan of Canada, a division of Canada Publishing Corporation.

A CIP catalogue record for this book is available from the British Library.

Microsoft Press books are available through booksellers and distributors worldwide. For further information about international editions, contact your local Microsoft Corporation office. Or contact Microsoft Press International directly at fax (206) 936-7329.

Acquisitions Editor: Lucinda Rowley

Project Editor: Ina Chang

Technical Contacts: Dail Magee and Kurt Meyer

FIELD GUIDE TO

PCs

Stephen L. Nelson

The Field Guide to PCs is divided into 4 sections. These sections are designed to help you find the information you need quickly.

1 ENVIRONMENT

Terms and ideas you'll want to know to get the most out of personal computers. All the basic parts of personal computers are shown and explained. The emphasis here is on quick answers, but most topics are cross-referenced so that you can find out more if you want to.

Diagrams of key personal computer components, with quick definitions, cross-referenced to more complete information.

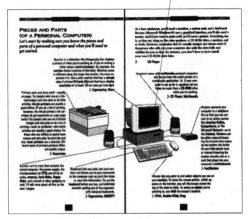

Tipmeister

Watch for me as you use this Field Guide. I'll point out helpful hints and let you know what to watch for.

Definitions of key concepts and terms and examples showing you why you should know them.

Quick identification of tools.

Step-by-step guides to performing most personal computer tasks.

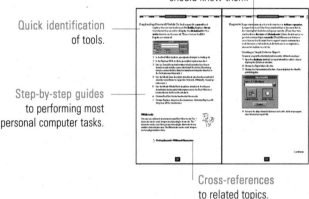

Cross-references to related topics.

INTRODUCTION

In the field and on expedition, you need practical solutions. Fast. This Field Guide provides just these sorts of lightning-quick answers. But take 2 minutes and read the Introduction. It explains how this unusual little book works.

WHAT IS A FIELD GUIDE?

Sometime during grade school, my parents gave me a field guide to North American birds. With its visual approach, its maps, and its numerous illustrations, that guide delivered hours of enjoyment. The book also helped me better understand and more fully appreciate the birds in my neighborhood. And the small book fit neatly in a child's rucksack. But I'm getting off the track.

This book works in the same way as that field guide. It organizes information visually with numerous photographs and illustrations. And it does this in a way that helps you more easily understand and, yes, even enjoy working with your personal computer. For people contemplating buying a new personal computer, the Field Guide provides lots of advice and tons of tips for getting the right personal computer—and stretching your dollars the farthest. For new users, the Field Guide provides a visual path to the essential information necessary to start using a personal computer running Microsoft Windows 95. But the Field Guide isn't only for beginners. For experienced users, the Field Guide provides concise, easy-to-find descriptions of the tasks, terms, and techniques you need to know about using your personal computer and Windows 95.

HOW TO USE THIS BOOK

Let me explain how to find the information you need. You'll usually want to begin with the first section, Environment, which is really a visual index. In Environment you find the picture that shows what you want to do or the task you have a question about. Say you're looking for a new personal computer and want to know what all you need to buy. You can flip to pages 2-3, which shows an illustration of a personal computer system.

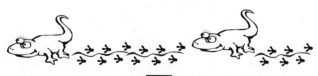

Next you read the captions that describe the parts of the picture—or key elements of a personal computer system. Suppose, for example, that you can't figure out how to choose a monitor. The picture box on pages 2-3 shows captions that describe each of the parts of a personal computer system—including the monitor. These key elements appear in **boldface** type to make them stand out.

You'll notice that some captions are followed by a little paw print and additional **boldface** terms. These refer to entries in the second section of this book, Personal Computers A to Z, and provide more information related to the caption's contents. (The paw print shows you how to track down the information you need. Get it?)

Personal Computers A to Z is a dictionary of more than 200 entries that define terms and describe tasks. (After you've worked with your personal computer a bit or if you're already an experienced user, you'll often be able to turn directly to this section.) So if you have just read the caption that says you want a monitor that has a **refresh rate** of at least 60 **hertz (Hz)**, you can turn to the "Hertz (Hz)" entry in Personal Computers A to Z and learn what in the world the term "hertz" means and why the "refresh rate" (whatever that is!) is important.

When an entry in Personal Computers A to Z appears as a term within another entry, I'll **boldface** it the first time it appears in that entry. For example, as part of describing what a **disk cache** is, I tell you it's part of a computer's **memory**. In this case, the word memory appears in boldface letters—alerting you to the presence of a "Memory" entry. If you don't understand the term or you want to do a bit of brushing up, you can flip to the entry for more information.

Here's one other really important point. Don't forget about the Index. It provides another way for you to find what you're looking for. So if you can't find a term in the Environment section or in Personal Computers A to Z, use the Index. You'll probably find the term there.

The third section, Troubleshooting, describes problems that new or casual users of personal computers often encounter. Following each problem description, I list one or more solutions you can employ to fix the problem.

The Quick Reference section does a couple of things. It provides a worksheet that you can use to document your personal computer's configuration, or guts. I suggest you fill out this worksheet so that you'll have a permanent copy of the stuff that's packed into your PC. (If you're buying a personal computer, ask the salesperson to help you fill out this worksheet.) The Quick Reference section also lists **technical support** telephone numbers for a bunch of hardware manufacturers and software developers. Having all of these numbers in 1 place can be handy. If you travel with your personal computer, for example, you only need to carry only 1 little book: this Field Guide.

CONVENTIONS USED HERE

I have developed 3 other conventions to make using this book easier for you. First, rather than using wordy phrases such as "Activate the File menu, and then choose the Print command" to describe how you choose a command, I just say "Choose the File Print command."

Second, in a few places, I talk about toolbar buttons that you click to start certain tasks. Rather than say "Select the Save toolbar button from the Standard toolbar," I simply say "Select the Save tool." (Whenever I do this, I show a picture of the toolbar button in the margin, too.)

And third, to describe how you find and start applications or find and open documents using the Start menu, I tell you to click the Start button, and then I list in order the menu items you choose. For example, I might say, "Click the **Start button,** and then choose Programs, Accessories, System Tools, and Backup." I think this approach works much better than the more precise but also very wordy alternative, "Click the Start button. Then choose Programs from the Start menu, choose Accessories from the Programs **submenu,** choose System Tools from the Accessories submenu, and, finally, choose Backup from the System Tools submenu."

ENVIRONMENT

Need to get the lay of the land quickly? Then the Environment is the place to start. It defines the key terms you'll need to know and the core ideas you should understand as you consider buying or you begin using your personal computer.

PIECES AND PARTS
(OF A PERSONAL COMPUTER)

Let's start by making sure you know the pieces and parts of a personal computer and what you'll need to get started.

Monitor is a television-like thingamajig that displays a picture of what you're working on. If you're writing a letter using a **word processor,** for example, the **monitor** shows a picture of the letter. Monitors come in different sizes; the larger the monitor, the more expensive it is. Get a color monitor that has a **refresh rate** of at least 60 **hertz (Hz)** and that has a display **resolution** of at least .28 mm dots per inch (dpi).

❧ **Ergonomics; Glare**

Printers print and draw stuff—usually on paper. For people who are on a limited budget and who plan to do little printing, **ink-jet printers** are usually a good choice. (If you do a lot of printing, however, the ink-jet printer's ink cartridges do get expensive on a per-page basis.) For people who are on a limited budget and who plan to do a lot of printing—such as students—dot matrix printers are usually a good choice. For those who are willing to spend more money and who plan to print lots and lots, **laser printers** are a safe bet. Different types of printers produce different quality output.

❧ **Resolution**

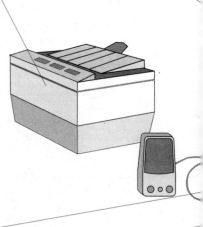

System unit is a box that contains the actual computer: the power supply, the microprocessor (or **CPU**) and all its circuitry, **memory, hard disks, floppy disks,** and a bunch of other gadgetry as well. I'll talk more about all this on the next 2 pages.

Keyboard lets you enter text and numbers and allows you to give commands to the computer such as *print this letter* or *save this information.* Try out the **keyboard** before you buy, and definitely consider getting one of the ergonomically designed keyboards.

❧ **Ergonomics; QWERTY**

At a bare minimum, you'll need a **monitor,** a **system unit,** and a **keyboard.** Because Microsoft **Windows 95** uses a graphical **interface,** you'll also need a **mouse.** And if you want to print stuff, you'll need a **printer.** Everything else is, as they say, icing on the cake: speakers, a CD-ROM drive, a modem, and so forth. However, remember that it's usually cheaper and always easier if the person who sells you your computer also adds the extra bells and whistles for you so that, for instance, you don't have to try to install your own CD-ROM drive later.

⁘ CD Player

Speakers come with **multimedia** personal computers and let you hear the audio portion of a multimedia application. Or, if your computer is set up for it, speakers let you listen to music from a **CD-ROM** drive while you're working.

⁘ CD Player; Multimedia

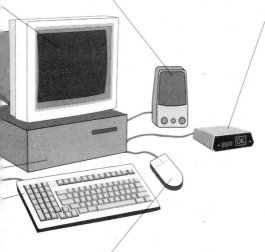

Modem connects your computer to a telephone line so that you can connect to an online service like **America Online, CompuServe,** or The **Microsoft Network**—or to the **Internet.** Modems can be either external (meaning the circuitry that makes up the modem sits inside its own little plastic box) or internal (meaning the modem circuitry sits on a card that plugs into your computer's **motherboard**).

⁘ Fax/Modem

Mouse lets you point to and select objects you see on your **monitor.** To move the mouse pointer, which appears on the monitor, you slide the mouse across the top of the desk or table. To select an **object** you're pointing to, you **click** the mouse's buttons.

⁘ Click; Double-Click; Drag

WHAT'S INSIDE THE SYSTEM UNIT

It's what's inside the system unit, or box, that really counts. So if you're thinking about buying a computer or want to better understand the computer you already own, it's helpful to look under the cover.

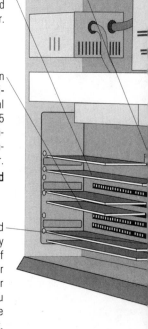

Microprocessor, or **CPU**, is the engine that powers your personal computer. It makes calculations and manipulates chunks of data. Most personal computers use **microprocessors** made by Intel Corporation, such as the 80386, 80486, and Pentium (or 80586) families of microprocessors. The higher the number, the more powerful the microprocessor.

Sound cards play music and other audio signals (such as speech) so that the sounds can be heard on speakers attached to the computer.

Graphics cards assist the microprocessor, or **CPU**, in doing the hard work of displaying stuff on your **monitor**. Graphics cards usually have their own special memory for storing whatever you or Windows 95 want to display on the monitor. You can buy a computer that does not have a graphics card, but a graphics card makes your computer run much faster.

⁘ **Expansion Board**

Memory, or RAM, is the temporary storage area used by the microprocessor as it runs. **Memory** is usually measured in **megabytes (MB)**; the more megabytes of memory your computer has (up to 16 megabytes or so), the faster your computer will run. Whatever information is stored in memory is lost when you turn off your computer unless you first save the information on a disk.

⁘ **Byte; Files**

A variety of components make up the system unit, but the 3 most important components are the **microprocessor** (the brains), the **memory**, and the storage devices (like hard disk drives, floppy disk drives, and **CD-ROM** disc drives). Most computers made nowadays also have a couple of increasingly important components: graphics cards and **sound cards.**

In addition to these core components, there are a bunch of odds and ends that most personal computers have: **parallel ports** and **serial ports,** or sockets, into which you plug things like **printers, modems,** and mice; the power supply; and the metal chassis into which all this stuff gets plugged and screwed.

⁂ Bay; Expansion Board; Expansion Slots

Floppy disks are removable storage areas (as opposed to fixed, permanent storage areas). To use a floppy disk, you insert the disk into a floppy disk drive. Floppy disk space is usually measured in either **kilobytes (KB)** or **megabytes (MB).** Typical floppy disk sizes are 360 KB, 720 KB, 1.2 MB, and 1.44 MB.

⁂ Byte; Labeling Disks

CD-ROM discs are also removable storage areas, but your computer doesn't write information to a CD-ROM disc. It only reads information from the CD-ROM disc. This characteristic, plus the fact that a CD can store more than a whopping 600 MB of information, makes CD-ROM discs the favorite storage choice of multimedia publishers. To use a CD-ROM disc, you insert the CD into a CD-ROM disc drive.

⁂ CD Player

Hard disk is the fixed, permanent storage area that your computer uses to store the software it runs (such as the **operating system** and any **applications**) and the information you want to keep (such as correspondence, business documents, and financial records). Hard disk space is also usually measured in megabytes. Whatever is stored on a **hard disk** remains stored when you turn off your computer. Typically, hard disk sizes are 100 MB, 200 MB, 500 MB, and even 1000 MB.

⁂ Byte

How to Buy a PC

*Once you've decided you want a personal computer,
your next step is to choose the right one to buy.*

1 Determine your requirements. Before
you even start looking at advertisements, consider what you want
to do with your new personal
computer. What you want
to do will determine the
software you need (or
want); the **system
requirements** of that
software will
determine what
kind of computer
you should buy.

2 Set a budget.
Don't be afraid to set
a budget. At this writing, you can
purchase awesome computing
power for just over a thousand
bucks. And prices keep falling.

3 Test drive. Be sure to try out the
software you'd like to use, either
at a retail store or at a friend's,
on a personal computer like
the one you might buy. At
the very least, doing this
will ensure compatibil-
ity between the
hardware and
software. More
importantly, however,
this testing will ensure that the
personal computer you're eyeing will
do the job you need it to do.

❖ Mail Order

Although the sheer number of computer manufacturers, retailers, mail order sellers, and advertisements can be overwhelming, it's actually quite easy to pick a personal computer because all **IBM compatible computers** use the same half-dozen or so basic components, or building blocks. For the average user, this means that there isn't any relevant difference in technology. You can instead focus on considerations such as price, reputation of the manufacturer and retailer, convenience, and service.

 Apple Macintosh; Product Reviews

4 Pick your PC. Get a personal computer that has at least a 486DX-66 **microprocessor,** a minimum of 8 MB of **memory,** a **hard disk** with 200 MB of storage space, and an SVGA **monitor.** If your budget allows, you'll never be sorry if you buy a **Pentium** that has more memory (up to 16 MB) and a larger disk (up to 500 MB).

 Byte

Setting up your PC

Setting up your computer is mostly a matter of finding a table or desk to hold the system unit, monitor, and keyboard and then plugging in the **cables.**

You'll be plugging in 2 kinds of cables: data cables (cables that transfer information, or data) and **power cords.** You'll need to plug in data cables that connect the system unit with the **monitor,** the **printer,** the **keyboard,** the **mouse,** the speakers, and the **modem.** You'll also need to plug in power cords for the monitor, the system unit, the printer, and, if your modem is external, the modem.

The **system unit** power cord should be plugged in last—and preferably into a **surge protector.** Once you plug this in, you can turn on your computer.

UNDERSTANDING SOFTWARE

Without software, your computer is essentially an expensive paperweight. It's the software that turns your computer into a tool.

Word processor software lets you write letters, reports, and other **documents.** Most word processor software also includes other helpful writing tools such as spelling checkers, grammar checkers, and form letter generators.

🐾 **Clip Art**

Game Software turns your personal computer into a toy, an amusement park, or a fun-filled learning tool. Some of the games applications even use **multimedia.**

🐾 **Educational Software; Games**

Spreadsheet software lets you manipulate tables (that is, rows and columns) of data. If you wanted to prepare a personal or business budget, for example, you would use spreadsheet software.

Catch-all software

There's a hybrid **software** category called "integrated software" that combines some features of most of the types of software described on this page. Microsoft Works, for example, does most of what **word processor,** spreadsheet, **database,** and telecommunications software does. This jack-of-all-trades-but-master-of-none approach is fine for people who don't need to fully exploit the feature set of a powerful, standalone word processor, spreadsheet, or database application.

The relationship between **software** and a computer is roughly like the relationship between the music on a cassette tape or compact disc and a stereo. Just as a cassette tape or compact disc stores the music that a stereo plays, software stores the instructions a computer needs to work—to do things like display pictures on a **monitor,** write and read information from a **disk,** and do word processing or accounting tasks.

Data management software helps you store, organize, and retrieve information. If you wanted to build a list of thousands or even tens of thousands of names and addresses, for example, you would use database management software.

Accounting software and personal finance software track a business's and an individual's financial affairs.

Telecommunications software lets you connect your computer (using a **modem**) to another computer or to a **network.**

❖ Linking Computers;
   Online Services

Operating System works directly with your computer. It's the operating system, for example, that displays images on the **monitor** and writes and reads information from a **disk. Windows 95** is operating system software. So is **MS-DOS.**

❖ OS/2; UNIX

"Word processor" is a misleading name

The name "word processor" is misleading because word processor software usually lets you include things beside words in a document. All of the popular word processors, for example, let you include pictures and tables.

PERSONAL COMPUTERS A TO Z

Maybe it's not a jungle out there. But you'll still want to keep a survival kit close at hand. "Personal Computers A to Z," which starts on the next page, is just such a survival kit. It lists in alphabetic order the tools, terms, and techniques you'll need to know.

America Online ⁖ Online Services

Any Key Occasionally your computer asks you to do something and then "press any key." But don't start looking for a key that's labeled "any." "Any key" means any one of the roughly 100 keys on your **keyboard**. You can press Enter. Or the O key. Or the K key. Or almost any other key. (You sometimes can't press keys such as Shift or Control.) You get the picture. Pressing a key simply tells the computer that you've done what it has asked you to do and that you're ready to get going again.

For example, if a **floppy disk** is in the disk drive when you turn on your computer, your computer sometimes can't start. When this is the case, you'll see a message that says:

```
Non-system disk or disk error
Replace and press any key when ready
```

Take out the floppy disk, and press any key on the keyboard. I know that suspicious types don't like to press the SysRq key (the one next to F12). No one knows what this key is for, and rumor has it that pressing this key, like stepping on a crack, will break your mother's back.

Apple Macintosh The computer world is divided into two camps, the Apple Macintosh camp and the **PC** camp. "PC" stands for "personal computer," and although Macintoshes are also personal computers, the term "PC" always refers to IBM computers and IBM compatible computers.

This book deals exclusively with PCs. You won't find anything here about Apple Macintosh computers, or "Macs," as they're called by their loyal users.

⁖ **IBM Compatible Computers**

Applications Applications are the programs that come with your computer or that you buy down at the software store or through the mail. They do such work as word processing, accounting, or creating spreadsheets and **databases.**

Microsoft sells several well-known and popular applications, including Microsoft Word (a word processor application), Microsoft Excel (a spreadsheet application), and Microsoft Access (a database application). There are lots of other popular and well-known applications; WordPerfect, Lotus 1-2-3, and Quicken are just a few of them. In this book, by the way, I'll always refer to these software programs as "applications."

There is also such a thing as an "applet." An applet is simply a small application. For example, **Windows 95** comes with several applets, including Calculator, WordPad, and HyperTerminal—all on the Accessories **submenu.**

This is Windows 95's Calculator applet.

Archiving Archiving means putting data in storage so that nothing can harm it and you can get to it later—perhaps years later, if need be. Not all data needs to be archived. Most users back up all their data and then set aside what's really important for the archives. In a business, for example, receipt records would be kept in an archive, but copies of business letters likely would not be.

continues

Archiving *(continued)*

Now that you know what archiving is, let me tell you why it's important: Some storage media are not suitable for archiving. Tapes can be used for backing up data but not for archiving because tapes can go bad after a few weeks. **Floppy disks** and **hard disks** are the best places to keep archives. (Some removable hard disks, for example, are guaranteed not to go bad for 5 years.)

❖ **Backing Up**

Arrow Keys

Most **keyboards** have 2 sets of arrow keys—some on the numeric keypad and one to the right of the Ctrl key. The keys point up, down, left, and right. Press these keys to move the cursor 1 line up or down or 1 character left or right on the computer screen.

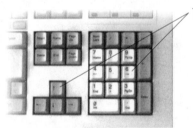

These are the arrow keys.

If you get numbers instead of a moving cursor

If you press an arrow key on the numeric keypad and you get numbers instead of a moving cursor, it means the Num Lock mechanism is on. Press the Num Lock key (it's right above the 7 on the numeric keypad) to turn this mechanism off. Now you can move your cursor using the arrow keys.

❖ **Cursor Keys; Toggle Key**

AUTOEXEC.BAT

AUTOEXEC.BAT is the name of a very important **file** in **MS-DOS** and in earlier versions of the Windows **operating system,** prior to **Windows 95.** Here's why AUTOEXEC.BAT is important in MS-DOS systems: It lists a bunch of commands—basically, warm-up exercises having to do with your **hardware** and the operating system—that your personal computer needs to run as it warms up. Windows 95 doesn't really need your AUTOEXEC.BAT file's list of commands to run. It knows what it needs to do to get going. But out of deference to the traditions of the past and so that you can run any old MS-DOS and old Windows **applications,** Windows 95 does look at the AUTOEXEC.BAT file. If AUTOEXEC.BAT is doing some warm-up exercises that Windows 95 doesn't do, Windows 95 automatically executes those commands. (See where the file gets its name? AUTOmatically EXECutes.)

And now we've spent more of your time on this old subject than is necessary. To be quite honest, the main thing you should know about the AUTOEXEC.BAT file is that if you have Windows 95 you don't need to know anything about AUTOEXEC.BAT.

❖ **CONFIG.SYS**

Backing Up

Backing up means making a second, temporary copy of a file so that you don't lose any data if something happens to the original file. Most computer **applications** can make backup files automatically. Automatic backup files, however, are stored on the **hard disk** along with original files. If something happens to the hard disk—if it crashes or is stolen or is eaten by gypsy moths—the backup files are rendered worthless along with everything else.

continues

Backing Up *(continued)*

The best place to store backup copies is on a **floppy disk.**
Once the backup is made, you can put the floppy disk in
an out-of-the-way place where nothing will harm it. Businesses sometimes use tape drives to make backups, but
that is another story. And one that often has a tragic end-
ing because tape drives aren't as reliable as floppy disks.

How often should you back up files?

The standard answer is "every time you finish working with one," but let's be re-
alistic. You're supposed to check your oil whenever you buy gas, too. Back up a
file whenever reconstructing it would be a hassle or a tragedy or when you
wouldn't be able to remember what you just put in it.

Backing Up a File on a Floppy Disk

The easiest way to back up a file is to copy it to a floppy disk using
Windows Explorer:

1 Put a floppy disk into the floppy disk drive.

2 Open Windows Explorer. To do this, click the Start button, choose
Programs from the Start **menu,** and choose Windows Explorer.
Click Windows Explorer.

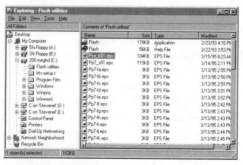

3 In the left side of the window, click the folder that holds the file
you want to back up.

4 In the right side of the window, click the file you want.

5 Choose the File Send To command, the fifth item down on the menu.

6 From the File Send To **submenu,** choose the floppy disk drive
you're copying the file to. You'll see a little cartoon of a piece of
paper flying between 2 folders.

7 Remove the disk from the floppy disk drive, put a label on the disk describing what's on it, and put the disk in a safe place.

You can save the file on a floppy disk, too

If you're working with an application that lets you save files (or **documents,** or whatever) using a File Save or File Save As **command,** you can also just save the file on a floppy disk. To do this, choose the File Save As command. Then use the Save In **drop-down list box,** which appears at the top of the Save As **dialog box,** to indicate that you want to save the file on the floppy disk drive.

Putting a Backup File Back on the Hard Disk

If an original file gets damaged, you can use its backup version by copying the backup from a floppy disk to the hard disk:

1 Put the floppy disk that holds the backup file into the floppy disk drive.

2 Open Windows Explorer by clicking the Start button, choosing Programs, and then choosing Windows Explorer.

3 In the upper left corner of the screen, click the floppy disk drive **object** that represents the disk drive in which the backup disk has been inserted. On the right side of the screen, you'll see the backup files that are on the floppy disk.

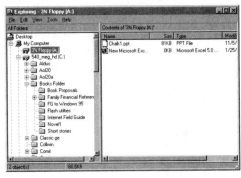

4 Click and drag the backup file (on the right side of the screen) to the folder (on the left side of the screen) that holds the original file.

5 Drop the file into the folder. You'll probably see a message that asks whether you want to replace the existing file with the backup file.

6 Click Yes. You'll see the flying piece of paper again.

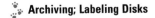

 Archiving; Labeling Disks

Bandwidth is the amount of data that travels on a communications line during, say, 1 second. For example, in the case of computers, you can use bandwidth to measure how much data travels from one computer to another computer in a given time interval. The bandwidth is measured in bits per second (bps).

Baud Baud (rhymes with Maude) is a measure of data-transmission speed. When it comes to modem speeds, people often talk about the "baud rate," although modem speed is not measured in bauds. Actually, modem speed is measured in the number of data **bits** that can be transmitted in a second. That is, modem speed is measured in bits per second (bps).

❖ **Modem**

Bay When you're talking about personal computers, a bay, or drive bay, is simply a shelf that you use to put things like **floppy disk** drives, **hard disk** drives, tape drives, and **CD players**. The number of bays a **PC** has is important because it's one of the factors that limit your ability to add new **hardware** to the PC. So unless you buy your PC with every bell and whistle you'll ever want, you probably want to get a computer that has a free bay. Or even 2 or 3 free bays. If you're thinking about adding, say, a CD player to your PC, you need to have a drive bay for the **device;** otherwise, you have to opt for a device that is external to your PC and connects with a **cable.**

These are bays.

BBS

BBS stands for bulletin board system. In essence, BBSs work like those cork bulletin boards you see at the local grocery store—the ones that hold messages advertising ancient Winnebagos for sale, 12-year-old kids who want to baby-sit, and rewards for finding lost dogs.

The only difference with a BBS is that you post and read these messages electronically, by using your computer and a **modem.** You use a communications application like **Windows 95's** HyperTerminal to connect to the BBS. If you want to do this, the best approach is to just call the BBS operator and ask how you're supposed to connect.

BIOS

I'm including this term only because you sometimes hear people use it. You don't really need to know anything about the BIOS or ever worry about it. You don't need to know that the term stands for Basic Input Output System, for example. And you don't need to know that the term is pronounced "Bye-Ohss." That said, I will tell you that the BIOS is essentially a simple set of instructions that get your computer going and ready for the operating system, **Windows 95.**

Bit

Bit stands for "binary digit." A bit is the amoeba of computer data. It is the smallest unit. Each bit represents a 1 or a 0. Bits are grouped in bunches of 8 to form **bytes,** and bytes represent real information, such as letters and the digits 0 through 9.

Modem transmission speeds, by the way, are measured in bits per second (bps).

Bit-Mapped

Bit-mapped **fonts** and graphics are similar to Navajo sand paintings—they are composed of many dots. Taken together, the dots form shapes, letters, or patterns. The dots correspond to **pixels** on your screen. If you zoom in on a bit-mapped graphic, you can see the dots. Paint, the accessory application that comes with **Windows 95,** stores images as bit maps. Try zooming in on a Paint **file** sometime to see how it is bit-mapped. Here you see a picture of a bit-mapped font—in this case, the letters W, a, and y.

Way **Way**

🐾 **PostScript; TrueType Fonts**

Bleeding-Edge Technology

Some people like to be on the cutting edge of technology. If they're buying a new personal computer, they want the very fastest **micropro-cessor,** the most newfangled video card or **modem**, and the most breathtakingly huge **hard disk** available. I under-stand all this technolust. I'm human. I'm not immune to the seductive powers of 150-megahertz microprocessors. But let me offer a friendly observation for any new or be-ginning computer users: The cutting edge of technology is also often the bleeding edge of technology. And in my experience, you're most likely to run into weird technical problems if you're buying cutting-edge technology. For this reason, I suggest that you not buy any new hardware gizmo until it's been out on the market for a few months and the inevitable new-product kinks have all been ironed out.

By the way, I'm much less concerned about the bleeding edge of technology for **software**. Software publishers like Microsoft Corporation, Lotus Development Corporation, and Novell, Inc. test their newest software on tens of thousands of guinea pig users before they release it. So it's these poor fools—not you—who do the bleeding if there's any bleeding to be done.

Board

Boards hold the silicon **chips** and other electronic components of the **system unit** in place. Each system unit has a **motherboard.** (The motherboard is the board that holds the **microprocessor.**) A system unit might have other kinds of boards as well. An internal **fax/modem** requires a fax board before it will work. A memory board gives the computer additional **memory.**

Boards are called boards, by the way, because there really is a plastic board—it looks sort of like a little sheet of plywood. And it's into this board that all the board's components plug.

❖ **Daughterboard; Expansion Board**

Booting ❖ **Turning On Your Computer**

Bug

A bug is a problem that causes **software** to produce incorrect results or to malfunction. Computer applications are "debugged" before they are put on the market. To "debug" means to test software for errors and then fix them.

Bulletin Board System  BBS

Bus   The bus is part of a computer's circuitry. It moves data to and from the **CPU**. **Expansion boards** can be added to the bus to make the computer more useful. There are different standards for the kinds of expansion boards you can add. If you plan to add an expansion board, be sure you know which type of standard your computer uses:

Bus	Description
EISA	Extended Industry Standard Architecture, an advancement on the ISA standard.
ISA	Industry Standard Architecture, the most common standard. It was developed for the IBM PC/XT.
MCA	Micro Channel Architecture, used on the IBM PS/2. It's faster than EISA and ISA.
Local	Lets you plug **boards** straight into the **motherboard.** It's fast.

 **Expansion Slots**

Byte

A byte is the basic unit of computer data. Each byte is composed of 8 **bits** and is the equivalent of 1 letter or 1 digit from 0 to 9. File sizes, disk space, and **memory** are all measured in bytes.

When you start adding Greek prefixes like "kilo" and "mega" to the word "byte," you get new words and a whole lot more than 1 byte:

Word	Total bytes	Rough total	Abbre-viation	Example
kilobyte	2^{10} (1024)	1 thousand	KB	150 words—or roughly a page of text
megabyte	2^{20} (1,048,576)	1 million	MB	A 500-page thriller, a la Tom Clancy
gigabyte	2^{30}	1 billion	GB	A thousand 500-page thrillers—or roughly the number of books needed to fill up 5 of those floor-to-ceiling bookcases
terabyte	2^{40}	1 trillion	TB	A million books or more—10 times the number of books available at a big bookstore
petabyte	2^{50}	1 quadrillion	PB	It boggles the mind

Cables

Until the advent of the cordless computer, which probably will arrive at about the same time as the cordless extension cord, computer users will have to tangle with cables. Not counting the cords that go in the wall socket and the monitor cable that comes with a **monitor** (so you don't have to worry about it), 3 kinds of cables are attached to personal computers:

Cable	Description
Network	Network cables connect the network **cards** of computers in a, duh, **network.** If you're shopping for a network cable, be sure that you know which kind of connector sockets the cable should have. The cable's connector sockets need to match the network card sockets.
Parallel	Parallel cables connect your computer's **parallel ports,** or sockets, to some other piece of **hardware**—usually a **printer.** Parallel cables are pretty much all the same, so if you need a parallel cable you can just trot down to the local computer store and buy one.
Serial	Serial cables connect your computer's **serial ports** to some other piece of hardware, such as an external **modem** or a **mouse.** A serial cable can have a couple of different connectors, so you'll need to look carefully at the sockets into which you'll plug the serial cable to be sure you get a cable that has the right size sockets and the right number of pins. You almost always have to buy cables when you buy a computer system. Ask the salesperson to help you get the right ones.

Cache Memory

Cache **memory** refers to high-speed memory **chips** located on the system **board.** Data that you access often is stored temporarily in cache memory. Cache memory saves processing time because the computer can simply reach into cache memory for data instead of having to rummage around in normal memory, which takes longer.

Cache memory runs up to 5 times faster than normal memory.

 Disk Cache

C

Card   Cards are the little **boards** that you plug into the
motherboard of a computer so that your computer can
do more things. **Sound cards,** for example, provide better
sound and the ability to play music and **games.** "Card" is
just another name for "**expansion board.**"

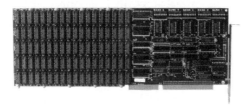

A card.

.·. **Expansion Slots**

Carpal Tunnel Syndrome .·. Ergonomics

CD Player   CD Player is the name of an application that comes
with Windows 95. As you can probably guess, it lets you
play audio CDs using a CD-ROM drive. Sometimes
people also call the CD-ROM drive a "CD player." And
that's OK.

Windows 95 comes with
the CD Player application,
which looks and works
like the one you usually
play music on.

Want to add a CD player to your computer?

Before Windows 95, it was murderously difficult to add a CD player to a PC.
There were all sorts of ugly things you had to do to get the darn thing working
right. But nowadays things are much, much different. If you want to add your own
CD player and you know how to use a screwdriver, you're all set. All you need to
do is be sure that you get a CD player that's labeled "Windows 95 Plug and Play."

CD-ROM "CD-ROM" stands for compact disc read-only **memory.** On a CD, the data is stored and read using laser light. Most people are familiar with audio CDs, but CDs can also store reference material, periodicals, multimedia **games,** and computer **applications.** A single disc can hold over 600 **megabytes (MB)** of information, roughly the equivalent of 1,800 360-KB **floppy disks.** However, you cannot put your own information on a CD—that's why it's called "read-only."

This is a CD-ROM disk.

To play a CD-ROM on your computer, you need a **CD player** (also called a "CD-ROM drive"). CD players will soon be standard equipment on computers. They'll be right in the system unit next to the floppy disk drives. In the meantime, if you want to play CDs you need a CD player. You can plug one into your system as you would any other **peripheral.**

To make the most of the new CD-ROM medium, get a double-speed CD player that conforms to MPC-2, the standard for playing multimedia discs. I also recommend a 16-bit **sound card** that can translate what's on the CD-ROM discs into a sound signal for speakers. And if you want to go the whole hog, get good speakers, too.

 Bit

Check Box   Check boxes are on-off switches. On your computer screen, they often look like little squares. If a check box is turned off, the little square is empty. If a check box is turned on, the little square shows a checkmark.

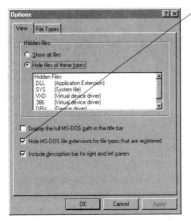

Windows 95 uses little checkmarks to mark check boxes, as do many Windows-based applications.

Chips   Chips are the silicon crystals that most of your computer's circuitry are packed into. If you drop a computer in an aquarium, you get fish and chips. (Not really.)

    CPU; Math Coprocessor

Click   To click means to tap a **mouse** button once, quickly and authoritatively. To pull down a **menu** and see the **commands** it has to offer, you click its menu name. You click the screen to move the text cursor to a new location. You click the **scroll bar** to scroll your **file** to a new place. There are as many things to click on a monitor screen as there were cliques back in high school.

continues

27

Click *(continued)*

If you can't figure out how to click

Don't feel bad if you can't figure out how to click your mouse. A couple of years ago, I got a little laptop. But I could not figure out how to click its mouse. I examined the mouse in minute detail. I fiddled and faddled with it for days. Deeply humbled, I called the store where I bought the computer. Disguising my voice, I asked the salesperson how to click the mouse. It turned out that the main mouse button was on the side of the mouse and that it looked like the mouse's label. No wonder I couldn't find the thing. The moral of this little story is that if you can't figure out how to click your mouse, call the place where you bought your PC or mouse.

 Double-Click

Clip Art   Clip art refers to the pictures that you can paste into documents. Many word processors and drawing packages come with clip art images.

This clip art image comes with Microsoft Word. In keeping with the jungle-adventure motif of this book, I selected an elephant.

Clone   When the personal computer was in its infancy, all **PCs** were made by IBM. However, they were quite expensive, so young entrepreneurial daredevils working with soldering irons started making clones. Clones worked almost as well as PCs, but they didn't have the IBM stamp of approval.

You don't hear the term "clone" much anymore. Nowadays, lots of respectable manufacturers clone the IBM PC. These big shots did not want their computers to be called "clones," which sounds too much like "clowns," so a new term had to be coined. That new term was "**IBM compatible computer.**" If your PC was not made by IBM and it's not an **Apple Macintosh,** it's a "compatible" and not a "clone."

Closing Applications ❖ **Stopping Windows-Based Applications**

Closing Files ❖ **Files**

Closing Windows ❖ **Window**

Combo Box "Combo box" sounds like a special order from a fast food take-out place. But it's not. A combo box is a hybrid **dialog box** element that is part **text box** and part **list box.** You can, therefore, enter something in a combo box the way you enter something in a text box. Or you can activate a **drop-down list box** and select an entry from it.

This is a combo box. You can enter something in this box, just as if it were a text box. Or you can activate the drop-down list and select one of its entries.

Command Buttons

Command Buttons Command buttons tell Windows-based **applications** that you either are or are not ready to do something. For example, every **dialog box** shows a command button that's labeled "OK." If you click the OK button, the Windows-based application knows that you're ready to move forward. So clicking OK is your way of giving the Windows-based application the thumbs-up signal.

Most dialog boxes also show the Cancel command button. Cancel means, basically, thumbs down.

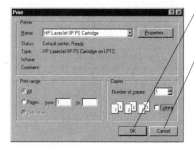

To choose the OK command button, simply press Enter.

To choose the Cancel command button, click it.

Choosing Command Buttons

To choose a command button, you can use any of three methods: You can click the button using the **mouse.** Or you can use the Tab and Shift+Tab keys to highlight the command button with a dark border and then press Enter. (If the button already shows a dark border, you can simply press Enter.) Or if one of the letters in the command button name is underlined, you can hold down the Alt key and press the underlined letter.

Displaying additional options

If the text on a command button is followed by greater-than symbols (>>), clicking the button expands the currently displayed dialog box. If the text on the command button is followed by an ellipsis (...), clicking the button displays another dialog box. For example, the Properties command button in the last screen picture includes an ellipsis (Properties...).

Commands You issue commands to applications to tell them what you want them to do. For example, "Microsoft Word, I command thee to print this letter!" Unfortunately, you can't issue commands verbally yet. You use the following procedure:

Edit	View	Insert	Format
Can't Undo			Ctrl+Z
Repeat Formatting			Ctrl+Y
Cut			Ctrl+X
Copy			Ctrl+C
Paste			Ctrl+V
Paste Special...			
Clear			Del
Select All			Ctrl+A
Find...			Ctrl+F
Replace...			Ctrl+H
Go To...			Ctrl+G
AutoText...			
Bookmark...			
Links...			
Object			

1 Click the name of a **menu** in the menu bar near the top of the screen, or press Alt and the underlined letter in the menu name. A menu drops down.

2 Choose the command using one of these 3 methods: Click the command name, type the underlined letter in the command name, or use the Up and Down arrow keys to highlight the command name and then press Enter.

Disabled commands are grayed out

A grayed-out command cannot be chosen because the application either doesn't have enough information to carry it out or because you're working in a part of the application to which the command doesn't apply.

 Dialog Box

Compatible "Compatible" means that **hardware** made by different manufacturers can work together. It also means that **software** from different developers can work together. And it means that hardware and software from different manufacturers and developers can work together.

Hardware manufacturers and software developers want their stuff to work with as many different **devices** and kinds of software as possible because compatibility means more customers. That is why most software for the **PC** is compatible with **Windows 95** or with **MS-DOS**. It's also why word processor **applications** work with most types of printers.

However, some products are not compatible. When you shop for computer hardware, software, and **peripherals,** be sure that everything you buy is compatible with everything else.

❖ **IBM Compatible Computers**

CompuServe ❖ **Online Services**

CONFIG.SYS As its name implies, the CONFIG.SYS **file** contains information about how the computer's system is
configured. With **Windows 95,** your computer doesn't
really need a CONFIG.SYS file. But it keeps one around
anyway for the same basic reasons that it keeps an
AUTOEXEC.BAT file around. In fact, in a broad
brushstroke sort of way, you can think of a CONFIG.SYS
file as similar to an AUTOEXEC.BAT file. The
CONFIG.SYS file may list some special programs,
called "**drivers,**" that your computer needs to start as
it's warming up.

I'm not going to spend any more time on this
CONFIG.SYS business. You really don't need to worry
about it with Windows 95. One thing I will tell you,
however, is that you really shouldn't fool around with a
CONFIG.SYS file unless you thoroughly understand the
system drivers you're fiddling with.

Configure To configure a computer system means to let it know
what its various parts are so that the parts can work together correctly. In the past, configuring a computer was
an onerous task best left to a technical witch doctor, but
nowadays most **applications** configure themselves when
you install them. In fact, **Windows 95** includes a capability called "Plug and Play," which means that as long as
the various pieces of **hardware** are Plug and Play enabled,
Windows 95 takes care of all the hardware configuration.

∴ **CONFIG.SYS**

Control Panel Have you ever seen a news video of a nuclear
reactor? You know how there's always a room with a
bunch of people wearing white coats and hard hats and a
big, huge control panel with a bunch of lights and
switches and gauges?

continues

Control Panel *(continued)*

Windows 95 has a similar Control Panel that controls the way Windows 95 operates. Fortunately, you don't need to be a nuclear engineer to use Windows 95's Control Panel. To change one of these settings, you just open Control Panel (such as by clicking the Start button and next choosing Settings and then Control Panel). Then you click the appropriate Control Panel tool.

To change some aspect of how your computer works, you use one of these tools.

Copying Files ✧ Files

Copying or Moving Data Between Documents

In Windows-based **applications,** there are 2 ways to copy or move data from one **document** to another. You can use the Clipboard, or you can use the drop-and-drag method. To learn how to use the drop-and-drag method, refer to the **drag** entry.

Copying or Moving Data Using the Clipboard

The Clipboard is a holding tank in which you can store data. Whatever is on the Clipboard is inserted in a **file** when you click the Paste button or choose the Paste command from the Edit **menu.** To copy or move data between documents using the clipboard:

1 Drag the **mouse** over the data you want to copy or move. The data will be highlighted.

2 If you're going to copy the data, click the Copy button, or choose Copy from the Edit menu. If you're going to move the data, click the Cut button, or choose Cut from the Edit menu. Now the data is on the Clipboard. (The Clipboard is hidden, so you can't actually see the data.)

3 Go to the place in the second document that you want to copy or move the data to.

4 Click the Paste button, or choose Paste from the Edit menu..

Drag; OLE; Window

Copyright According to copyright law, you cannot use someone else's images or "intellectual property" without their permission. The McDonald's golden arches, a picture of the starship *Enterprise*, Bart Simpson's head, "Howl" by Allen Ginsberg, and even Vanna White's face are copyrighted. If you invented a video game in which Bart Simpson and Vanna White recited "Howl" and rode the starship *Enterprise* to a faraway planet where people worshipped the golden arches, you would violate several copyrights.

In the computer world, the subject of copyrights comes up in 2 areas: First, any of the **software** you buy is copyrighted, which means that although you can (physically) make copies for all of your friends, you may not do so legally. If you have questions about what you may or may not do, see the software license agreement that comes inside each software package. Second, this copyright business also concerns **clip art.** Sometimes you can use the art as you see fit. But sometimes you can use it only so long as the thing you're using it for will not be sold for profit. Because of the differences in licensing rules, you should check the licensing agreement that comes inside the clip art packaging.

Shareware

CPU

CPU stands for "central processing unit." The CPU is the brain of the computer. It makes all computations, gives instructions, and interprets instructions from computer **applications.** The CPU is also called a "microprocessor." It resides on a **chip** inside the system unit.

CPU speed is measured in **megahertz (MHz).** You will have a rough idea of how fast your CPU is if you know what its megahertz rating is. And if you were brave enough, you could open the system unit and see the CPU chip. It has a number on it, such as 80286, 80386, or 80486, or a name, such as **Pentium.** (You might call a Pentium an "80586.")

You can think of these microprocessor numbers—80286, 80386, 80486, and 80586—as roughly equivalent to an engine's horsepower. The bigger the number, the more horsepower a car or truck has, and the more cargo the car or truck can carry around. So roughly speaking, the difference between an 80486 running at 33 MHz and a Pentium (or 80586) running at 90 MHz is equivalent to the difference between a 1-ton pickup truck that goes 33 miles per hour and a 2-ton pickup truck that goes 90 miles per hour. Not only does the faster pickup truck zip around at much greater speed, but it also carries twice the load.

By the way, if your current computer is an 80486 microprocessor running at any speed—25 MHz, 33 MHz, or whatever—you're in good shape. You've got plenty of horsepower on your hands. (If the computer's performance seems slow, your cheapest and best solution is just to add more **memory.**)

If you're going out to buy a new computer, you'll want to get at least an 80486 microprocessor running at 66 MHz. And if your budget allows, you'll probably never be sorry if you buy a Pentium microprocessor or whatever comes after the Pentium. (Do read our little digression on **bleeding-edge technology,** however.)

 **Math Coprocessor**

Crash   If you're discussing PCs, the term "crash" refers to either of a couple of incidents. If an application or the operating system wipes out and stops working, this wipeout is called a "crash." And if a hard disk fails and you can't read data from and write data to it anymore, this failure is also called a "crash."

Curb Feeler   Before about 1963, luxury cars were fitted with curb feelers on them. A curb feeler was an antenna-like device attached to the right-rear fender of the car. It was designed to help in parallel parking. When you backed the car close to the curb, the curb feeler scraped the cement and made a loud scratching noise. That's how you knew you were close to the curb and should stop backing up, lest you scratch the chrome on the fender. An ingenious device. I wish cars still had them.

 Tube

Cursor   The cursor is the thing on the screen that indicates where the **mouse** pointer is or where text will appear if you start typing. There are 5 types of cursors:

Cursor	What it does/looks like
⧗	This is the Wait cursor. It isn't really a cursor, but it appears on the screen when the computer wants you to wait until it completes a task. It looks like an hourglass.
I	This is the Mouse pointer cursor. This cursor looks like an I-beam. It moves on the screen when you roll the mouse around.
⇖	This is the **Selection cursor**. When you roll the I-beam cursor over something that can be selected, it turns into the Selection cursor. This cursor looks like an arrow.
✛	This is the Move cursor. When you're moving something, you see this cursor on top of whatever you're moving.
↙ ↘ ↔ ↕	These are the Resize cursors. These cursors appear when you try to drag a border or a grid. The diagonal ones are for moving the corner of the border or grid; the others are for moving the top, bottom, or sides.

Keyboard

Cursor Keys

The cursor keys are the keys you press to move the cursor. On enhanced **keyboards,** there are 2 sets of cursor keys. One set is on the numeric keypad, and the other is just to its left, beside the Ctrl and Enter keys. Here are the cursor keys:

Key	Moves the cursor
↑	One line up
↓	One line down
←	One space or cell to the left
→	One space or cell to the right
PgUp (Page Up)	To the previous on-screen page
PgDn (Page Down)	To the following on-screen page
Home	To the beginning of the line
End	To the end of the line (sounds ominous)

🐾 **Arrow Keys**

Cutting-Edge Technology 🐾 Bleeding-Edge Technology

Daisy-Wheel Printer
A daisy-wheel **printer** works like a typewriter. Keys on a daisy-wheel printer strike a ribbon and make impressions on the paper below. The daisy-wheel printer is almost obsolete. So you don't want to buy one. But if someone will give you an old one for free, go ahead and take it.

Database
A database is a collection of data arranged into well-defined categories. Your address book is an example of a database, even if it's not in a computer. In an address book, data is arranged in 7 distinct categories—last name, first name, street number and name, city, state, ZIP code, and telephone number.

Users of **data management software** can manipulate the information in computerized databases in many ways. For example, they can get lists of people in a particular state. Or they can find items in an inventory that fall in a certain price range and fit a certain description.

You might not know it, but your name and address are in countless databases. No doubt you have received plenty of junk mail. You received it because your name and address are in address list databases. Your credit history is kept in a database. Utility companies keep your payment history in a database. A good sleuth could probably write your biography by examining the databases your name is in.

Data Management Software

Data management **software** is used to store and keep track of information in **databases.** The software is used for inventories, payrolls, address lists, and other kinds of record keeping. To get the big picture and see how their businesses or finances are doing, users can get summary "reports" of what is in a database using this software.

Data management software can also arrange, or "sort," data in many different ways. For bulk mailings, the software allows addresses to be arranged in ZIP code order and printed on labels, making it easier for the post office to sort the envelopes. A marketing company can use data management software to target individuals in high-income area codes. Or a company selling locust insurance can use the software to send mass mailings to people in locust-infested states.

Examples of data management software include dBASE, Microsoft Access, Paradox, and Quattro Pro. Let me also say, however, that if you just want to create and maintain a simple database, all of the **integrated applications** have less powerful but very useful data management tools.

Daughterboard

A daughterboard is an **expansion board** you can attach to—what else?—the **motherboard** of a computer to give the computer more performance, power, and functionality. Among other things, daughterboards can provide video support, **modem** capability, and more **memory** to a computer system.

This is a daughterboard.

dBASE ⁂ Data Management Software

Defaults Defaults are the choices that computer **applications** think you're most likely to make. For your convenience, applications offer default choices so that you can just press Enter or click the OK button to select them. If you want to go against the grain and make choices different from the defaults, you have to fiddle around a bit.

The default Page Range choice is all the pages.

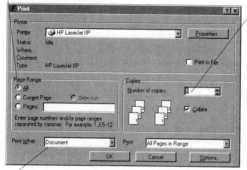

The default Copies choice is 1 copy.

The default Print What choice is the entire **document**.

If you wanted to print 1 copy of the entire document, you could just press Enter or click OK in this **dialog box** and be done with it. But if you wanted to print 2 copies of pages 14 through 17, for example, you would have to abandon the default choices and change the settings in this dialog box.

Deleting "Deleting" is the arcane computer term for "erasing." The rubbery thing on the end of a pencil is not called a "deleter," but computer manuals always ask you to "delete" things. If you want to wipe **files** or **folders** off a **disk**, for example, you "delete" them.

Deleting Files ⁘ **Files**

Deleting Folders ❖ Folder

Desktop The desktop is the background that appears beneath the application windows.

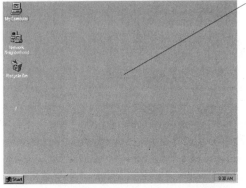

This background is the desktop.

Your desktop's appearance depends on the desktop pattern you've selected and the wallpaper you've said Windows 95 should use to "paper over" the desktop pattern. (This is strange, right? Wallpaper on a desktop? I agree.)

You specify a desktop pattern or wallpaper using Control Panel's Display tool.

 Shortcut Icons

Desktop Publishing Desktop publishing, or DTP for short, is a relatively new field. In the past, a typesetter, a layout artist, and sophisticated printing equipment were needed to create newsletters, books, pamphlets, posters, magazines, and the like. Now these materials can be created using desktop publishing **software** and a **laser printer.**

Desktop publishers can create sophisticated page layouts, headlines of various sizes, newspaper columns, figure boxes, and just about anything else that can be printed. For example, we use a desktop publishing **application** called PageMaker to create this and all the other Field Guides.

Microsoft Publisher and QuarkExpress are 2 other examples of desktop publishing software. Most word processors have desktop publishing capabilities as well. Microsoft Word and WordPerfect, for example, offer sophisticated fonts and page layout tools.

Graphics Applications

Device A device is something you plug into your computer. A good rule of thumb is that if this pluggable thing has a cable or screws, it's a device. (Otherwise, it isn't.) For example, tape drives, internal and external modems, floppy disk drives, and **printers** are all either screwed in or cabled. So they're devices.

Dialog Box A dialog box is an on-screen form you fill in to tell **Windows 95** or some Windows-based **application** how it should complete some **command.** Any command name followed by an ellipsis (...) displays a dialog box.

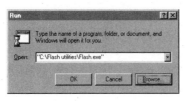
This is a dialog box.

Defaults

Directory   In **Windows 95,** the directory has been replaced by the **folder.** So instead of organizing **files** in directories, Windows 95 organizes files in folders. Now when you save a file, you choose a folder in which to save it instead of a directory.

If you worked with previous versions of Windows or with **MS-DOS,** you might want to think of folders as equivalent to directories. If you're new to the world of computers, however, you should just ignore this whole discussion.

Disk   Computers use disks for storage purposes. **Applications** and **files** are stored on **hard disks** and **floppy disks.**

Most computers have 1 or 2 **slots** in the front of the system unit for inserting floppy disks. If you could reach into one of these slots (but don't do it!) and yank out what's inside, you would see a disk drive like the one in the photograph. The disk drive reads what is on the floppy disk and sends it on to the computer. It also takes information from the computer and puts it on floppy disks.

This is a floppy disk drive.

You insert floppy disks into this slot.

Disk Cache

The disk cache is part of a computer's **memory**. Data that you stored recently and data that you're likely to need soon are kept in the disk cache so that the computer can get its hands on it faster.

For example, suppose you're word processing a **document** and you've been using 24-point Times Roman characters for the headings. When you save your document for the first time, the computer has to go rummaging through the **hard disk** to find the **files** it needs to display and print 24-point Times Roman. But once it has the files, it reasons that it might need them again soon, so the computer puts the files in the disk cache, where it can get at them faster. Next time you write a heading and save the document, it gets saved faster because your computer grabs the point size and Times Roman font information from the disk cache instead of from the disk.

🐾 **Cache Memory**

Disk Compression

I don't want to bum you out. But I need to tell you something. Eventually, my friend, your hard disk is going to fill up. Fortunately, Windows 95 gives you a way to both monitor the situation and correct it.

continues

Disk Compression *(continued)*

Finding Out How Much Hard Disk Space You Have

To see how much space is still available on your hard disk:

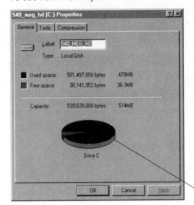

1 Click the Start button, and then choose Programs and **Windows Explorer.**

2 Click My Computer in the upper left side of the window.

3 In the Contents **window** on the right side of the screen, click the hard disk **object.** Most likely that will be C.

4 Choose the File Properties **command.** You'll see a pie chart that shows how much disk space is free and how much is occupied.

Using the DriveSpace Disk Compression Application

One way to economize on hard disk space is to use a disk compression application. Compression applications shrink the **files** on a hard disk by removing redundant information. Stacker is one such application. **Windows 95** comes with a disk compression application called DriveSpace.

To use DriveSpace:

1 Display the Properties dialog box as described in the previous section on finding out how much hard disk space you have available.

2 Click the Compression tab.

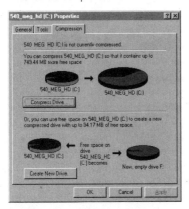

3 Click Compress Drive.

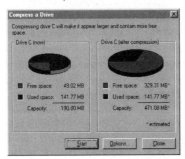

4 When Windows 95 displays the Compress A Drive **dialog box,** click Start.

A caution for people who have slow computers

If your **microprocessor** isn't working very hard—and this is likely with a fast microprocessor—disk compression won't slow down your computer one bit. But computers that have slow microprocessors don't work as well when their hard disks have been compressed. Here's the reason: A microprocessor has to go to quite a bit of work to scrunch and unscrunch information. If your microprocessor is already so overworked that it's slowing down, performance will only get worse if you ask it to take on the extra work of disk compression.

Utility Software

Display Adapter The display adapter is the electronic gadgetry inside the computer that's responsible for sending video signals to the **monitor.** Sometimes the display adapter is found on the **motherboard,** and sometimes it is included as an **expansion board.** Some people also call the display adapter a "video adapter."

Documents A document is a **file** created by a word processor **application** or some other application, such as a spreadsheet application. When it comes to copying, moving, or **deleting** documents, you can treat them like files. So just refer to the File entry. It describes how you do all of these things.

DOS DOS (rhymes with "boss") stands for disk **operating system.** When you turn on a computer, the first thing it does is kick-start itself by running DOS. In fact, that grinding sound you hear when you turn on a computer is the sound of the computer loading DOS. DOS controls everything in your computer and makes everything work together harmoniously.

Some technical stuff about the different versions of DOS

Usually when people talk about DOS they mean **MS-DOS,** the disk operating system put out by Microsoft Corporation. However, there are other versions of DOS. IBM sells something called PC-DOS, which you could think of as MS-DOS's cousin. (As you might guess, if your computer is manufactured by IBM, you've got PC-DOS.) And then there's another version of DOS called DR-DOS, which is put out by Novell, Inc. (Just so you know, you pronounce DR-DOS as "dee-are-dos" and not as "Doctor DOS.") DR-DOS works like MS-DOS but is actually a completely different operating system. **Windows 95** replaces all the various versions of DOS.

DOS Prompt ⁙ **MS-DOS Prompt**

Dot-Matrix Printer Dot-matrix **printers** are really inexpensive. You can get one for about $250. At reasonable print speeds, the print **resolution** is low—about 180 dpi (dots per inch). But for people on a budget with lots of printing to do, dot matrix printers are a good value. (You can also print at resolutions higher than 180 dpi, but the print speed slows down tremendously.)

Dot Pitch Dot pitch refers to the distance between the **pixels** on the screen. The pixels are the dots of light that blend together to make up what you see. The closer the pixels are, the better the image is. If you're shopping for a **monitor,** keep in mind that a dot pitch of .28 mm or smaller is considered good.

Double-Click Double-click means to tap the mouse button twice, quickly and authoritatively. There are many things to double-click in **applications.** For example, you can double-click a **file** shown in the **Windows Explorer** window to open it.

Rodent troubles?

If your **mouse** isn't double-clicking right, you can change its double-click speed. In **Windows 95,** click the **Start button,** and then choose Settings and Control Panel. In Control Panel, double-click Mouse. The Mouse Properties **dialog box** appears. Click the Buttons tab if it isn't already selected, and adjust the double-click speed in the bottom of the dialog box.

⁙ **Click; Drag**

Download This odd-sounding word simply means to retrieve a **file** from a **network** or from an **online service** such as CompuServe or America Online. You request the file, it is transferred to you by **modem** or by **cable,** and you save it on your **hard disk.**

Sometimes you hear the word "upload." Upload means to put a file on a network or an online service so that others can fetch it.

Drag To drag means to grasp something using the **mouse**—a text block, a **file,** an **icon,** or an **object,** for example—and move or copy it to a new location. Here's how:

1 Position the mouse cursor over the item you want to drag. The **cursor** turns into an arrow.

2 Press and hold down the left mouse button.

3 Drag the mouse and the item you're dragging along with it to a new location. You'll see a "shadow copy" of the item you're dragging, as in the illustration here, which shows a file object being moved to a new **folder.**

4 Release the mouse button.

About drag-and-drop

You'll sometimes hear people refer to step 4 as "dropping." When you release the mouse button, the item you're moving or copying "drops." This whole process, in this case, is called "drag-and-drop." What I don't like about the term "drag-and-drop," however, is that it sounds similar to a hunting technique whereby the game is dropped, dragged to camp, and then eaten.

Drag-and-Drop ❖ **Drag**

Drawing Applications ❖ **Graphics Applications**

Drive Bay ❖ **Bay**

Drivers   A computer system's different parts, or **devices**, do not speak the same language. Indeed, the **mouse, monitor,** and **printer** are not on speaking terms. They have different jobs to do. How, then, do they communicate with one another?

The answer is drivers. A driver is a software **application** that tells one device what the code being sent to it from another device means. For example, printer drivers tell the printer what the boldface codes, line breaks, and other parts of a word-processed **document** are so that the printer can print them correctly. Mouse drivers interpret double-clicks and other mouse motions so that the computer can understand them.

CD-ROMs, modems, and other **peripherals** all come with software drivers so that your system knows what to do with these strange new devices. You shouldn't have to worry much about drivers with **Windows 95.** In the old days—before Windows 95—people had to fool around with drivers all the time.

❖ **CONFIG.SYS**

Drop-Down List Box

A drop-down **list box** is a list box that doesn't show its list until you tell it to. To tell a drop-down list box to display its list, either click the down arrow at the end of the box or select the list box and then press Alt+Down arrow key.

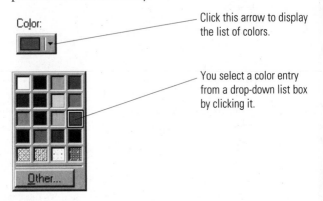

Click this arrow to display the list of colors.

You select a color entry from a drop-down list box by clicking it.

Educational Software

Educational **software** teaches people something. Much of the educational software is for children. Kids can learn spelling, arithmetic, or geography, for example, simply by sitting down in front of the family computer.

But this software category also includes some products for adults, too. One of the editors who works on the Field Guide series, for example, is brushing up on his Spanish before he heads off to Spain, learning key phrases such as "¿Donde esta el baño?" and "Triagame mas cerveza, por favor."

Electronic Mail ⁝ E-Mail

ELF Radiation

Is radiation from computers dangerous? Shoot, I don't really know. Computer **monitors** do emit ELF (extremely low frequency) radiation. Most people seem to think that ELF radiation doesn't hurt you, but no one knows for certain what the long-term effects are.

Before you get agitated about this, however, you should know a bit more: Most radiation from monitors is emitted by the back of the monitor and not by the front. Furthermore, the amount of radiation decreases dramatically with distance, so if you sit at least an arm's length away from the front of the monitor, you won't be exposed to very much radiation. If you're really worried about ELF radiation, get a **monochrome** monitor instead of a color monitor, or work on a **laptop.** Monochrome monitors emit far less radiation, and the liquid crystal displays on laptop computers emit no radiation at all.

🐾 **Ergonomics**

E-Mail

E-mail, which stands for "electronic mail," refers to the messages, love letters, notes, revelations, jokes, and party invitations that people on a **network** send to one another. An e-mail message is different from a **file.** E-mail is not saved on **disk**—unless you save it yourself after you finish reading it. (Files, on the other hand, can be sent over a network but are saved on disk.) E-mail usually shows up in a mailbox, is read and chuckled over, and is then discarded.

Members of **online services** such as CompuServe and The **Microsoft Network** can send e-mail to one another. E-mail can also be sent over the **Internet.**

Ergonomics

If you spend a lot of time in front of your computer, you are a candidate for back strain, eyestrain, and brain strain, not to mention Carpal Tunnel Syndrome. Nothing can be done about brain strain, but by taking a few simple precautions you can avoid injuries to your back, eyes, wrists, and arms.

Your Aching Back

Get an adjustable chair that is comfortable to sit in. You should be able to adjust the backrest and change the seat height. The main thing is to have lower back support because the lower back is where most strains from sitting in one place too long occur. If your shoulders and upper back ache, you may want to try an ergonomic **keyboard**.

This is Microsoft's ergonomic keyboard.

Avoiding Eyestrain

Glare on a **monitor** screen causes eyestrain. Keep the monitor out of direct light. If you can, keep the monitor in shadow, and use an adjustable light to illuminate whatever it is you're working with besides your computer and monitor. You can buy antiglare screens that attach to the monitor screen and cut down glare.

The monitor should be at eye level to encourage you to sit up straight. It should also be an arm's length away to avoid exposure to radiation.

Injuries to Wrists and Arms

Carpal Tunnel Syndrome, also called "repetitive motion injury" or "repetitive strain injury," is caused by swelling in the tendons in the wrists or by swelling in the synovial sheaths that surround those tendons. Swelling occurs when you hold your arms and wrists the same way for long periods of time and make repetitive actions—in this case, typing and moving the **mouse**. Tingling, numbness, and soreness in the wrists and forearms are symptoms of Carpal Tunnel Syndrome.

To avoid this injury, adjust your desktop and chair so that your elbows are higher than your wrists when you type. You can buy a keyboard holder that attaches to a desk and allows you to adjust the height of the keyboard. You can also buy a special mouse that reduces strain on the wrist. It looks like a soap dish and forces you to keep your wrist flat on the desktop.

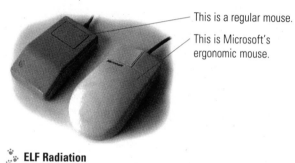

This is a regular mouse.

This is Microsoft's ergonomic mouse.

ELF Radiation

Expansion Board Expansion boards fit onto the **motherboard** of a computer to give the computer more functions and capabilities. They are also called "expansion **cards**" and "**daughterboards**." For example, an expansion board can be added to boost **memory**, give you an internal **modem**, provide video support, or add more **serial ports** or **parallel ports**.

This is an expansion board.

Expansion Slots

Expansion Slots Inside the system unit, computers have expansion slots where **expansion boards** can be plugged in. A PC can have anywhere from 3 to 12 expansion slots. Many or most of these slots are filled up with expansion boards right from the factory. So if you want to add some new gadget to your computer, you should first check to see whether there's an empty slot for you to plug the gadget into.

These are empty expansion slots.

If you're looking for a new computer and you think you're likely to add **devices** to your computer, you probably want some empty expansion slots. For most new users and home users, a couple of extra expansion slots will probably be more than adequate.

Fax/Modem   You can send faxes using a PC, but to do so you need a fax/modem. Fax/modems do the work of both fax machines and **modems.** They send and receive faxes, and they also send and receive **files** and **e-mail.** If you have a fax/modem, you can send any file on your computer to a fax machine. Incoming faxes are stored on your computer, and you can print or view them on the screen. To receive a fax, however, your computer must be turned on, and that means leaving your computer on into the wee hours of the morning if you expect to receive faxes then.

Keep in mind that you can only fax what's on your **hard disk** using a fax/modem. To fax found photographs and hand prints, for example, you need a scanner, too.

If you use a fax/modem, you may want to use the Microsoft Fax At Work **application.** It's built right into **Windows 95.**

Female Connector   A female connector is a connector with a hole or holes into which you insert another connector (with a plug or pins). The connector with the plug or pins is called, not surprisingly, a male connector.

Files   In computer land, you work with files. Data gets stored in files. **Applications,** or programs, are stored in files. When you begin work, you open a file. When you're finished, you save and close the file. The following are basic instructions for opening, saving, closing, creating and naming, copying, moving, printing, renaming, and deleting files. How to do these tasks varies a bit from application to application, but most Windows-based applications follow the same procedures.

continues

F

Files *(continued)*

Opening Files from Inside Applications

To open a file from inside an application:

1 Click the Open button on the toolbar, or choose the File Open **command.** You see the Open **dialog box.**

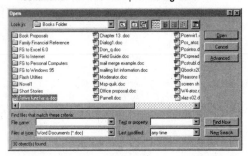

2 In the Folders (or Directories) box in the middle of the dialog box, scroll to find the folder that holds the file you want to open, and then click it. A list of the files that are in the folder appears in the File Name box on the left.

3 In the File Name box, double-click the file you want to open.

Opening Files Using Windows Explorer

To open a file using Windows Explorer:

1 Click the Start button. Then choose Programs and Windows Explorer.

2 In the All Folders **window** on the left side of the screen, click the folder that holds the file you want to open. All files in the folder appear in the Contents window on the right.

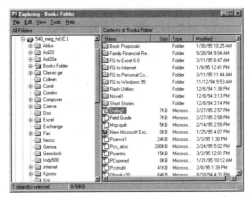

3 In the Contents window, double-click the file you want to open. Not only does the file open, but the application you created it in starts as well.

Opening Files Using Shortcut Icons

To open a file that's represented by a shortcut icon, just double-click the shortcut icon.

Saving a File

To save a file, click the Save button, or choose the File Save **command.** If you're saving a file for the first time, you see the Save As dialog box.

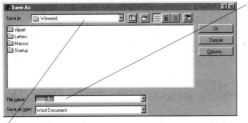

Type a name for the file in the File Name **text box.**

Using the Folders (or Directories) box, scroll and click until you find the **folder** you want to keep the file in. Then click OK.

continues

Files *(continued)*

Save files frequently

When you save a file, it gets put on your computer's **disk,** where nobody can touch or harm it. If the power goes out or if rats nibble through your computer's **power cord** and the electrical supply is cut, you'll lose all the work you haven't saved yet. So save often.

Closing a File

To close a file, choose the File Close command. If you haven't saved your work, the application displays a dialog box like this one to give you a chance to do so before you close the file. Click Yes in the dialog box if you want to save your work.

How the Close button works

You can close a file and an application at the same time by clicking the Close button (the one marked with an "X") in the upper right corner of the application window. You can also close just the file by clicking the Close button in the upper right corner of the document window.

Creating and Naming Files

To create and name a file:

1 Choose the File New command, or click the New File tool. A new, blank document window with a brand new file appears on the monitor screen.

2 Save the file. To do so, click the Save button, or choose the File Save command. Since you're saving a file for the first time, you see the Save As dialog box.

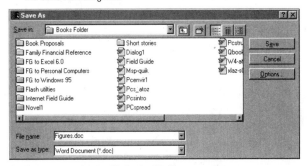

3 Type a name for the file in the File Name text box.

4 In the Folders (or Directories) box, scroll and double-click until you find the folder you want to keep the file in.

5 Click Save.

For the longwinded (or the Welsh)

File names can be 250 or so characters long and can be made up of any letters or numbers. You can also use blanks. And you can use most of the other characters you see on your **keyboard,** too, except for these:

" / \ [ ] : (* | < > + = ; , ?

The main thing is, you want to use a name that describes what's in the file. Think of a meaningful name so that years from now when you see the file name in a folder, you'll know what's in that file.

continues

Files *(continued)*

Copying a File

To copy a file to a new folder, to a floppy disk, or from a floppy disk:

1 Click the Start button, and then choose Programs and Windows Explorer.

2 In the Contents window, double-click around until you open the folder that has the file you want to copy. Or if you're copying a file from a floppy disk, click the **object** that represents the floppy disk drive. The files that are in the folder or on the floppy disk appear in the Contents window on the right side of the screen.

3 Click the file you want to copy to select it. If you want to copy more than one file, you can. Hold down the Ctrl key as you click each file you want to copy.

4 Choose the Edit Copy command.

5 Open the folder you want to copy the file to by clicking on its icon. Or if you're copying the file to a floppy disk, click the object that represents the floppy disk drive.

6 Choose the Edit Paste command.

Moving a File

To move a file to a new folder, to a floppy disk, or from a floppy disk:

1 Click the Start button, and then choose Programs and Windows Explorer.

2 In the Contents window, double-click around until you open the folder that has the file you want to move. Or if you're moving a file from a floppy disk, click the object that represents the floppy disk drive. The files that are in the folder or on the floppy disk appear in the Contents window on the right side of the screen.

3 Click the file you want to move to select it. If you want to move more than one file, you can. Hold down the Ctrl key as you click each file you want to move.

4 Choose the Edit Cut command.

5 Open the folder you want to move the file to by clicking its icon. Or if you're moving the file to a floppy disk, click the object that represents the floppy disk drive.

6 Choose the Edit Paste command.

Printing a File

 To print a file, either click the Print button on the toolbar or choose the File Print command. If you click the Print button, the file is printed immediately using the application's default settings. Using the defaults likely means that 1 copy of the whole thing is printed.

If you choose the File Print command, you can make choices about how to print the file. You can choose how many copies to print and which pages to print, for example, and make other choices besides, depending on the application.

Renaming a File

To rename a file:

1 Click the Start button, and then choose Programs and Windows Explorer.

2 Click around until the file you want to rename appears in the Contents window.

3 Click the file name 1 time to select it and then again to tell Windows 95 you want to rename it. (You can also click the file and object and choose the File Rename command.)

4 Type a new name, and press Enter.

Deleting a File

To delete a file:

1 Click the Start button, and then choose Programs and Windows Explorer.

2 Click around until you find the file you want to delete.

3 Choose the File Delete command

continues

Files *(continued)*

If you accidentally delete a file

If you delete a file and discover to your chagrin that you shouldn't have deleted it, look for it in the Recycle Bin. Deleted files stay there until you empty this bin. The "Troubleshooting" section of this Field Guide includes an entry called "You Accidentally Deleted a File" that describes how to get a file back from the Recycle Bin.

 Documents

Floppy Disk Floppy **disks** store **files.** To use a file on a floppy disk, you insert the disk into the appropriate slot on the front of your computer and tell **Windows 95** to read from the disk. At that point, a light in the front of your computer goes on, and you hear a grinding noise that sounds like cockroaches scuttling across linoleum.

Floppy disks have places on them for attaching labels so that you can write down what's on the disk and preserve that information for eternity. They also have "write-protect notches." Unfortunately, these write-protect notches work differently for 5¼-inch floppy disks and 3½-inch floppy disks. On a 5¼-inch floppy disk, when the write-protect notch is *closed* you can't alter or add to what's on the disk. On a 3½-inch floppy disk, when the write-protect notch is *open* you can't alter or add to what's on the disk.

According to computer lore...

A man once called the technical support department of a computer firm because he was having trouble getting his computer to read a 5¼-inch floppy disk. "Did you close the door on the disk?" the technical support person asked. A door slammed. "I just did," said the man, "and now the thing's bent way out of shape."

If you try to copy a file to a floppy disk and Windows 95 tells you there is a "Write Protect Error," the write-protect notch on the disk is "locked" (closed if the disk is 5¼ inches and open if the disk is 3½ inches). Unlock it if you do indeed want to copy something to that disk. For 5¼-inch floppy disks, peel the sticker off. And for 3½-inch floppy disks, slide the little square in the corner down.

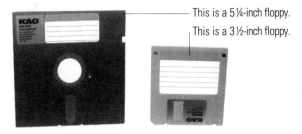

This is a 5¼-inch floppy.

This is a 3½-inch floppy.

Types of Floppy Disks

There are 2 types of floppy disks: 5¼-inch disks and 3½-inch disks. The 5¼-inch disks really do "flop." After you insert a 5¼-inch disk, you have to close the door—more like a latch, really—behind the disk before the computer can read what's on it.

The smaller 3½-inch disks do not flop at all. They are quite rigid and look a lot like beer coasters. All you have to do is shove them in, and when you want them back you push an eject button on the front of the computer similar to the eject button James Bond had in his Aston-Martin.

Besides differences in size, floppy disks are either "low density" or "high density." High-density disks have a higher storage capacity. The 5¼-inch high-density disks hold 1.2 **megabytes (MB)**, and the 3½-inch high-density disks hold 1.4 MB. If you try to read a high-density disk and your disk drive is built for low-density disks, you'll see a "General failure" message.

continues

Floppy Disk *(continued)*

The Right Way to Store and Handle Floppy Disks

Magnets harm floppy disks. They erase the data on them. Store floppy disks away from magnets, and that includes audio speakers, which have magnets inside them.

When you mail a 5¼-inch floppy disk, enclose it in a cardboard mailer so that it doesn't get bent, or else bury it deep inside whatever it is you're sending (and tell the recipient of the package where the floppy disk is hidden). These 5¼-inch floppy disks are dainty things. If you write on the label using a ball point pen, the pen can scratch the surface of the disk and render it useless. So use a felt tip pen.

Formatting Floppy Disks

You use **Windows Explorer** to format floppy disks. To format a floppy disk after you've started Windows Explorer and inserted the floppy disk in the floppy disk drive:

1 Right-click the floppy disk drive **icon.** Windows 95 displays a menu.

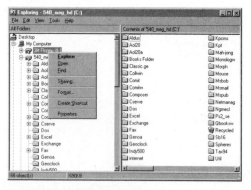

2 Choose Format. Windows 95 displays a **dialog box.**

3 Use the Capacity **drop-down list box** to select the correct floppy disk drive capacity. (If this sounds like Greek, or worse, like Geek, just read the floppy disk label. It'll probably give the floppy disk drive capacity.)

4 Optionally, use the Format Type **option buttons** to specify which type of format you want. If you don't know what you want here, let Windows 95 pick for you.

5 Click Start. Windows Explorer displays a progress bar at the bottom of the screen to show you the formatting operation's progress.

6 Click Close when Windows Explorer finishes—unless, of course, you want to format another disk.

Formatting hard disks

Never, under any circumstances, should you format a **hard disk.** If you do, you'll erase everything on it, after which there will be much pulling of hair and much gnashing of teeth. Formatting hard disks is something that only computer manufacturers and technical support people do. It's not for us ordinary folk.

Folder   Windows 95 uses folders to organize your **disks** and the **files** they store. (Folders, by the way, replace the **directories** used in older Windows versions.) You can also organize the files in a folder by creating folders within a folder. Basically, these folders work like the drawers in a filing cabinet. You can create folders and see which folders organize the files on a disk by using **Windows Explorer.** The following are the basic instructions for creating, deleting, moving, copying, and renaming folders.

continues

Folder *(continued)*

Creating a Folder

To create a folder:

1 Click the Start button, and then choose Programs and Windows Explorer.

2 Click the folder you want to place the new folder inside.

3 Choose the File New Folder **command.**

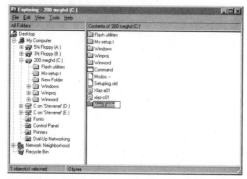

4 Type a name for the new folder.

5 Press Enter.

Deleting a Folder

When you delete a folder, you also delete all the files inside it. To delete a folder:

1 Click the Start button, and then choose Programs and Windows Explorer.

2 Click the folder you want to delete.

3 Choose the File Delete command. You see a message box that asks whether you really want to delete the folder by removing it and placing it in the Recycle Bin.

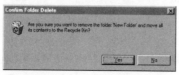

4 Click Yes when Windows Explorer asks if you really want to delete the folder.

If you make a boo-boo

If you delete or destroy a folder by mistake, most often you can get back its files. Open the Recycle Bin, and pull the files out. In the "Troubleshooting" section of this Field Guide, the entry called "You Accidentally Erased a File" describes **undeleting** files, and the same procedures work for undeleting folders.

Moving, Copying, and Renaming a Folder

You move, copy, and rename folders in the same basic way that you move, copy, and rename files. I describe how you do these things in step-by-step detail in the "Files" entry. So you'll want to look there if you have questions.

Fonts   A font is the complete collection of letters, numbers, and symbols available in a particular typeface, including all italicized and boldfaced variations of the letters, numbers, and symbols and all size variations. Technically speaking, a font is different from a typeface, but I've never understood the difference exactly, and anyhow the terms "font" and "typeface" are used synonymously. Just so that you understand this font business, here are some example fonts:

`This font is Courier.`

This font is Times New Roman.

This font is Helvetica.

   Bit-Mapped; PostScript; TrueType Fonts

Freeware   **Shareware**

Function Keys The function keys are the 10 or 12 "F" keys usually located along the top of the **keyboard.** On old keyboards, the function keys are located on the left side of the keyboard.

Different **applications** do different things with function keys. You press them by themselves or in combination with other keys to execute **commands.** In most applications F1 is the "Help key." You can press F1 to get instructions for using the application.

Games Enthusiasts believe that interactive entertainment in the form of games played on computers will be to the next century what movies were to this one. Maybe so. There are scads of computer games and scads of people playing computer games.

It's not easy to categorize the variety of games you can play, but here goes:

Type	Description
Arcade-style games	Doom is the most famous arcade-style game. In Doom, you run across the Martian landscape dealing murder and mayhem on the locals. Just by reading a list of the names of other arcade-style games, you'll get an idea of what's in this category: Terminator, Rampage, X-Wing, Jill of the Jungle, Kiloblaster, and Rebel Assault.
Classic games	These are PC versions of games like chess, solitaire, and poker. A lot of puzzle games and card games in this category are available for play when the boss isn't looking.

Strategy games	These are simulation games in which players must make thoughtful decisions to win. For example, in SimCity you play the part of a city planner and try to construct a healthy, happy city. In 2 games called Railroad Tycoon and Detroit, you must make business decisions for the success of a railroad and auto company. There's even a game called Pizza Tycoon in which the goal is to make yours the most successful pizza take-out chain in the land.
War games	An inordinate number of war games seem to be around. (If you think the average game player is male and age 20 to 40, you're dead right.) Some war games, such as X-COM and Master of Orion, borrow from science fiction and have the player defend the earth against invaders. Others, such as 1944: Across the Rhine, are historical.

GEnie ❖ Online Services

Gigabyte (GB) ❖ Byte

Glare Glare can be a big problem with **monitors.** Light from a lamp or especially from fluorescent ceiling lights bounces off the glass screen of your monitor and into your sensitive eyes. Ouch. If glare becomes too much of a problem, buy an antiglare screen. An antiglare screen covers the front of the monitor and cuts back on glare.

Graphics Applications

Graphics applications—also called "paint applications" and "drawing applications"—are for creating artwork on a computer. Most have tools that imitate the pencils, paintbrushes, stencils, and borders that artists use.

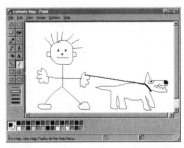

Windows 95 comes with a graphics application called Paint.

The great advantage of graphics applications is that you can use them to experiment, erase, tinker, putter, and dabble with a piece of artwork without having to continually start the piece all over again. Should the superhero's face be neon green or bright blue? With a graphics application, you can try it both ways and see for yourself which is best.

Some graphics applications are strictly for professionals. If you're shopping for a graphics application, look for one that matches your skill level. Here are a few other issues to consider:

Feature	Description
Drawing tools	A graphics application should have a good set of drawing tools to help you draw shapes and make patterns.
File formats	The application should support a variety of file formats since you'll likely export and import the artwork that you create to and from other applications.
Text and font manipulation	You should be able to twist, spindle, and rotate text in a variety of **fonts**.
Scanning	**Scanners** can capture images into bit-mapped **files**. If you'd like to use images from many different sources, get a graphics application that can use scanned files.

H

Need a graphics application?

CorelDraw, Windows Paint, and Windows Draw are excellent graphics applications. (Windows Paint, by the way, comes free with Windows 95.)

Hard Disk A hard disk, sometimes called a "hard disk drive," is the collection of revolving platters inside the computer that hold data **files.** A read/write head that is similar to a phonograph needle writes data to the revolving platters and reads data from them. A hard disk has 2 to 8 platters for holding data.

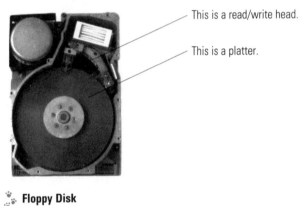

This is a read/write head.

This is a platter.

Floppy Disk

Hardware In computer terminology, hardware is anything that you can touch that has to do with computers. The computer itself, the **monitor,** the **keyboard,** the **hard disk,** the **CD-ROM** drive, the **printer,** and the **modem** are all examples of hardware. **Software,** on the other hand, is the stuff you can't actually get your hands on that makes the hardware run.

Help   All **applications** worth their name have online help. Usually the rightmost **menu** name on the menu bar is "Help." Click this menu when you need help using an application.

Windows 95's online help is both thorough and nifty. To use it, click the Start button and choose Help. You'll see a **window** that includes 3 tabs: Contents, Index, and Find.

When the Contents tab is displayed, you click a "book" to find information about a topic.

Using the Find tab, you can search for specific words or phrases that describe what you need information about.

Click the Index tab to see an index of help subjects. Once the Index tab is displayed, you type the name of the subject you're interested in, and the list below scrolls to that subject.

Hertz (Hz)   Hertz (Hz) is the unit for measuring frequency, equal to 1 cycle per second. "Frequency" simply means how often a periodic event occurs.

The only reason you need to have even an inkling about what hertz measures is that **CPU** speed and monitor **refresh rates** are measured in hertz and **megahertz (MHz)**. You don't really need to know that 1 MHz equals 1 million cycles per second. But you should know that the faster, or higher, the megahertz number, the better.

Home Finance Software ⁘ **Personal Finance Software**

IBM Compatible Computers

Any computer that works like an IBM PC but does not have the IBM label on it is an IBM compatible computer, or simply a "compatible." Compatibles use the same **software** and the same peripheral **devices** as IBM PCs. All compatibles can run **Windows 95,** for example. Packard Bell, COMPAQ, Tandy, and a host of other electronics firms make IBM compatible computers.

Besides IBM PCs and compatibles, the only other popular kind of personal computer is the **Apple Macintosh,** or "Mac." This book does not cover the Mac. All information in these pages deals with IBM personal computers and compatibles.

Clone

Icon

An icon is simply a visual image, or picture, that represents something else. **Windows 95,** for example, places icons on the **desktop** to represent shortcut routes, or **shortcut icons.** You'll also sometimes see an icon on a **command button.** And **Windows Explorer** (plus its little brother, My Computer) uses icons to represent the devices connected to your computer and the applications and other files stored on your disks.

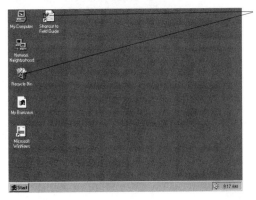

These are icons.

Object

Ink-Jet Printer Ink-jet printers work by spraying ink through little nozzles, or jets, onto the page. Ink-jet printers cost less than top-of-the-line **laser printers** and print almost as well. (You can get a good ink-jet printer for around $300.) However, ink-jet printers print more slowly than laser printers; they print at 1 to 4 pages a minute. Ink-jet printers are probably best for home offices rather than for businesses.

Inserting CD-ROM Discs There are a couple of different flavors of **CD players** or CD-ROM drives (or whatever you want to call them). With some of them, you press a button that tells the CD player to eject the tray that holds the CD-ROM disc. Then you place the CD-ROM disc in the tray and press the eject button again. Other CD-ROM players require that you use a caddy, or little box. With this variety, you place the CD in the caddy and then insert the caddy in the CD-ROM drive. To remove the caddy, you press the drive's eject button.

Inserting Floppy Disks To insert a 5¼-inch **floppy disk** in a floppy disk drive, you push the floppy disk into the drive **slot** and then, usually, turn a little handle to lock everything in place. Turning the little handle is also called "closing the door." (So when people say that you should "close the door" on a floppy disk, they don't mean that you should slam, like, your office door on it.) To later get the floppy disk out, you just repeat these same steps in reverse.

To insert a 3½-inch floppy disk in a floppy disk drive, you also push the floppy disk into the drive slot. But with these smaller floppy disks, there's no little handle that you need to turn to lock everything into place. When you want to get the floppy disk out later, you press the little eject button that's next to the slot.

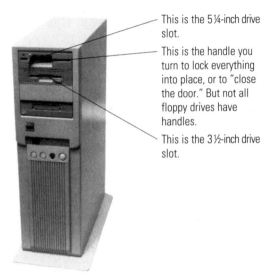

This is the 5¼-inch drive slot.

This is the handle you turn to lock everything into place, or to "close the door." But not all floppy drives have handles.

This is the 3½-inch drive slot.

Insertion Point The insertion point is the small vertical bar that shows where what you type gets placed. If this seems unclear to you, start a Windows-based application such as WordPad, begin typing, and look at the bar that moves ahead of the text you type. See it? That's the insertion point.

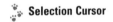 **Selection Cursor**

Installing Software There are 2 schools of thought about how to install **software.** One school says you should read whatever installation documentation comes with the software and then carefully and precisely follow those directions. If that sounds like a good idea to you, you should stop reading here. Instead, go find the product documentation, and start reading it.

continues

Installing Software *(continued)*

The other school of thought regarding software installation is to just wing it. I prefer the winging it approach because it almost always works and almost always saves time. If you'd like to join our little club, here's the new member's initiation: First, rip open the box the software comes in, and find the **floppy disks** or the **CD-ROM** disc. Don't worry about all that other stuff or the documentation—at least not yet. Second, insert the floppy disk that's labeled something like "disk 1" into the floppy disk drive. Or if the software installs from a CD-ROM disc, insert the disc into the CD-ROM drive. Then follow these steps to install the software:

1 Click the Start button, and then choose Settings and **Control Panel**.

2 In Control Panel, double-click Add/Remove Programs.

3 Click the Install button under the Install/Uninstall tab.

4 Sit back and follow any instructions you see on the screen. Whenever you're given choices and a **default** suggestion is provided, accept the default. And don't open the installation documentation unless you really get stuck.

Integrated Applications

An integrated **application** is a software program that lets you build spreadsheets, do word processing, create and fiddle with simple **databases,** communicate by **modem,** and sometimes do other tasks as well. Integrated applications are inexpensive, easy-to-use, "all-in-one" applications. An integrated application may be all you need or want if your computing needs aren't very sophisticated. Microsoft Works and ClarisWorks are the 2 most popular integrated applications.

Interface

"Interface" is one of those dreadfully ugly computer words. It refers to how you interact with your computer—the ways you tell your computer what you want it to do. **Windows 95** uses a graphical interface (also called a "graphical user interface"), for example, so you see lots of pictures and get lots of visual feedback when you use it.

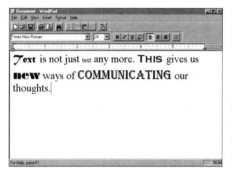

Windows-based applications use a graphical interface with lots of graphical imagery, overlapping **windows,** pull-down **menus,** and **icons.** You usually use a **mouse** to take advantage of all this stuff.

Text-based, or character-based, interfaces require you to type everything on the **keyboard.**

Interlacing Interlacing refers to the way your **monitor** draws items on the screen. An interlaced monitor makes 2 passes using an electronic beam that, in effect, shoots colors to draw what you see. A noninterlaced monitor makes only 1 pass.

This all probably sounds like the kind of technology stuff that's just too complicated for you to want to worry about. But it's actually important that you understand interlacing if you spend a lot of time in front of your monitor. Interlaced (or 2-pass) monitors are more likely to flicker. And that flicker often produces eyestrain and monstrous headaches.

 Refresh Rate

Internet The Internet is a worldwide information **network** of networks that, according to one estimate, links 3 million computers and 20 million users. Internet enthusiasts claim that information about virtually any subject is available somewhere on the Internet. The question is, how do you find what you're looking for?

The Internet began as a network for scientists and scholars to talk to one another and share computers, but now everyone is invited. Most North American and European universities and colleges maintain addresses on the Internet. And thousands of newsgroups (which work like bulletin board systems, or BBSs, but are always free of charge) are on "the net," where information can be exchanged and posted.

I could say a lot more about the Internet—but we don't have room here, so I'll simply let you know that Microsoft Press also publishes *Field Guide to the Internet.* (You can order this book by calling 1-800-MSPRESS.) I should say 1 more thing here, though, to parents. If your computer connects to the Internet either through an access provider or through an online service, you should know that there's a lot of sexually explicit material easily available on the Internet.

Joystick Some computer **games** require a joystick, which is a small pointing device that looks like a stick shift. Game players twist and bend their joysticks to kill aliens or make their race cars accelerate. To use a joystick, you need a joystick **port.** Joystick ports come on **expansion boards.** If you're thinking of buying a game that requires a joystick, get a joystick port if you don't already have one.

This is a joystick. If you buy a game that requires a joystick, you'll also need to buy a joystick port.

Keyboard   The keyboard offers your chief means of telling the computer what to do. On the keyboard, you'll find letters and numbers, **function keys,** calculator keys on the right side, and a few strange keys tucked in here and there.

The strange keys are gray. The table that follows shows what these gray keys do:

Key	What it does
|	This is the broken vertical bar, also called the "standpipe key." I mention it here because sometimes you're asked to press it, and it's nearly impossible to find. It's sometimes located above the Enter key.
~	This is the tilde key. It's also hard to find. Look for it in the upper left corner of the keyboard, below the Esc key. There's a pretty good chance it'll be there.
↑, ↓, ←, and →	These are the cursor-movement keys. Press them to move the cursor up, down, left, or right. One set of cursor-movement keys is found on the numeric keypad, and another is found to the left of the keypad, near the bottom of the keyboard.
Alt	Alt is a combination key that you press in combination with other keys to execute **commands.** For example, you might be asked to "press Alt+F4."
Backspace	Press this key to move the cursor backwards and erase characters on the screen.
Caps Lock	Press Caps Lock TO START TYPING UPPERCASE LETTERS. PRESS IT AGAIN to return to lowercase letters.
Ctrl (Control)	Like Alt, Ctrl is a combination key. You press it in combination with other keys to execute commands.
Del (Delete)	Delete erases characters to the right of the insertion point. One Del key is located below the 3 on the numeric keypad, and the other is located to the right of the Enter key.
End	Press this key to move the cursor to the right side of the screen.

Key	What it does
Enter	Pressing this important key tells the computer to do a command you've requested. In word processor **applications,** pressing Enter starts a new paragraph.
Esc	Pressing this important key tells the computer that you've changed your mind and want to stop what you're doing. You can often use this key to close a **dialog box** without doing anything and to deactivate **menus** you've just activated.
F1–F10 (or F12)	These are function keys. Press them to execute commands in an application.
Home	This key moves the cursor all the way to the left side of the screen.
Ins (Insert)	Press this key when you want to type over what's on the screen. When this key is pressed, the data you type replaces what's at the position of the cursor. Press the key again to turn off this overtyping and return to inserting the characters you type.
Num Lock	Press Num Lock when you want to use the calculator keys that are on the right side of the keyboard. After you press Num Lock, you'll get numbers (instead of moving the cursor) when you press the calculator keys. Press Num Lock again to return to using these keys to move the cursor.
PgDn (Page Down)	Press this key to move the cursor down 1 screen.
PgUp (Page Up)	Press this key to move the cursor up 1 screen.
Pause	When information is gliding across the screen so quickly you can't read it, press Pause. What's on the screen will lock in place. If you're lucky. Press Pause again to restart the action. Pause is the rightmost key on the top row of the keyboard.
Print Scrn	This copies whatever is on the screen to the Clipboard. In the old days, pressing Print Scrn sent everthing on the screen to the printer.
Scroll Lock	This key doesn't do anything. If you press it up and down real fast, you get the sound of mice running across floorboards.
Shift	Press Shift if you want to enter an uppercase character. Shift, like Alt and Ctrl, is a combination key. Sometimes you are asked to press it along with another key to choose a command.
SysRq	This key isn't used on a personal computer. Weird, huh?
Tab	This key enters a tab character. It moves the cursor to the next tab stop. In a dialog box, it selects the next text box or button.

continues

Keyboard *(continued)*

Most people use enhanced keyboards, but...

Most people use enhanced keyboards like the one shown in the preceding photograph. But a few old-fashioned AT keyboards are still in use. AT keyboards have the function keys on the left and 1 instead of 2 sets of cursor-movement keys. Other than that, the keys on an AT keyboard work in the same way as the keys on an enhanced keyboard. Then there is a thing called the "Dvorak keyboard," on which the keys are rearranged, supposedly to make typing easier. You'll know a Dvorak keyboard when you see one. On first sight, most people who encounter a Dvorak keyboard scratch their heads in bewilderment.

∴ **Arrow Keys; Cursor Keys; QWERTY; Toggle Key**

Keyboard Shortcuts Some menu **commands** have keyboard combinations such as Shift+F7 or Del or F8 next to them on the screen. These combinations are called "keyboard shortcuts." If you find yourself choosing a command often that has a keyboard shortcut, memorize the key combination, and start using it to give the command. You'll save time that way.

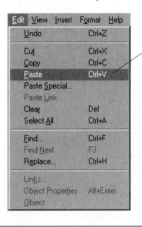

The keyboard shortcut for this Paste command is Ctrl+V.

Kilobytes (KB) ∴ **Byte**

Labeling Disks

Floppy disks have spaces at the top for attaching labels. If you can manage it, give your disks names that will mean something when you find them at the bottom of a drawer on moving day. More importantly, don't use a ball point pen to write on a 5¼-inch disk label (if the label is already affixed). Instead, write on the label before you affix it to the floppy disk or use a felttip pen.

Laptop

A laptop is a lightweight, shrunken-down computer that fits on your lap. Laptops themselves are shrinking. Now there are notebooks and subnotebooks as well. There is even a thing called a "palmtop." And somewhere, a poor soul is going blind trying to develop the first fingernailtop.

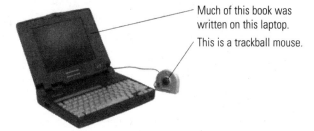

Much of this book was written on this laptop.

This is a trackball mouse.

The advantage of having laptops and their midget cousins is that you can take them on the road or to and from the office. Laptops take some getting used to, however. Some of the keys on a laptop keyboard are in different places than on a regular keyboard. And the screen can be difficult to read. Regular **monitors** work best in shadow where there isn't as much **glare,** but laptop screens are sidelit or backlit, and they work better in full lighting. Also, instead of a **mouse,** laptops have **trackballs,** which are little balls you roll with your thumb to move the cursor on the screen.

continues

Laptop *(continued)*

Most laptops use NiCd (nickel-cadmium) batteries, but these batteries tire quickly and are highly toxic. A better battery is the NiMh (nickel-metal hydride) rechargeable, which costs more but lasts far longer between recharges.

If you're shopping for a laptop or notebook, get one that has plenty of **memory** and hard disk capacity. On a regular computer, memory and hard disk space can be upgraded with **expansion boards,** but that often isn't true with laptops.

Most laptops have a **serial port** and a **parallel port** for plugging in a **printer,** as well as holes for connecting conventional **keyboards** and monitors in case you want to work with them. Look for the PCMCIA (Personal Computer Memory Card International Association) **slot** in the back of the laptop. This credit-card-sized device has a slot for a **modem,** hard drive, or expansion boards.

The jury is still out on the question of whether airport X-ray machines damage laptops. Instead of taking the risk, open your laptop for the guard to examine, and don't put it through the X-ray machine. By the way, you really can use a laptop on a plane—except during takeoffs and landings.

Using a laptop on a plane

If you often take a laptop on plane flights, get a flight simulation **game** like Jet or Flight Simulator. After the plane takes off, open your laptop, and start the game. Make like you're a real pilot. Make "vroom-vroom" airplane noises. When the other passengers start to squirm, turn to them and say, "Sorry folks, but it looks bad. There's a big storm ahead, and I don't think I can steer around it." OK, OK. Maybe this is not such a good idea...

Laser Printer A laser **printer** prints stuff on pages of paper in the same way that a photocopier does. You get great-looking output with a laser printer. But laser printers are also the most expensive printers you can buy. You're looking at several hundred dollars up to several thousand. Nevertheless, you get what you pay for. These babies usually support many different **fonts,** print graphics easily, and print fast—at 4 to 12 pages per minute. Oh, one other thing: For practical purposes, an LED printer is the same thing as a laser printer.

Buying paper for a laser printer

Anyone who tries to sell you paper designed especially for laser printers is pulling your leg. Photocopy paper works fine. Don't use erasable bond paper, however, because it has talc on it that can gum up a printer.

Learning Software ❖ **Educational Software**

Linking Computers Windows 95 lets you link, or connect, computers in several ways. If both your computer and the one you want to link to have network **expansion boards,** you network the 2 computers simply by connecting them with a **cable** and telling Windows 95 you want to network.

Using the HyperTerminal **application,** which comes with Windows 95, you can connect to other computers that have been set up as **bulletin board systems.**

If you've got a **laptop** computer, you can link it to another computer using the Direct Cable Connection application. (It appears on the Accessories **menu.**)

Windows 95 also includes special dial-up networking tools that let you connect to a **network**—such as the network at the office where you work.

continues

Linking Computers *(continued)*

None of this linking stuff is all that difficult. But if you're new to computers, you'll probably want to get some handholding from someone who's made such connections before. You can also pore over the documentation that comes with Windows 95 or get one of those big books on Windows 95. I recommend Craig Stinson's *Running Windows 95* (Microsoft Press, 1995)—and not because I like Craig or because the book is published by Microsoft Press. I just think Craig's book is best.

List Box If only a limited set of choices makes sense in a given situation and a Windows-based **application** knows those choices, it displays a list. Your life is then easier. All you have to do is select one or more of the list's entries.

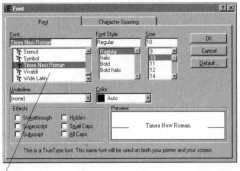

This list box shows **font** choices. You select a font either by clicking the font name in the list box or by using the **keyboard**.

Selecting a Single List Entry

You can select a single list entry by clicking it and then choosing OK. Or you can select a single list entry by highlighting it using the arrow keys and then pressing Enter.

Selecting Multiple List Entries

If you want to select more than 1 list entry—and if the application will
let you—you can do that, too. (This wouldn't make sense in the case
of a font choice, but it might make sense if you were selecting **files** to
open from a list.) You can select a contiguous range of list entries by
clicking the first list entry and then dragging the mouse to the last list
entry. You can also highlight the first list entry, hold down the Shift
key, and then press the Down arrow key to select additional list
entries.

If you want to select a noncontiguous set of list entries, hold down the
Ctrl key, and then click the entries you want to select.

Activating a Drop-Down List Box

If a Windows-based application doesn't have room to display a list
box—and this is usually the case—it uses a **drop-down list box.** In
this case, you don't see the list until you activate, or drop down, the
list by clicking its arrow.

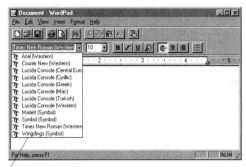

This is a drop-down list box.

Reviewing your choices

You can usually move to a list entry by typing its first character. For example, if
you're at the start of a list and are viewing the entries that begin with the letter
"A" but you want to move to the last part of the list and view the entries that begin with the letter "Z," type *Z*.

 Combo Box

Lotus 1-2-3 ⁖ Spreadsheet Applications

Mail Order

You can get inexpensive **hardware** and **software** by buying from mail-order houses. Mail-order houses offer a dizzying array of products at rock-bottom prices. However, if you need help installing or hooking up a product, a mail-order house in Palookaville, U.S.A. won't provide much help. And if the product is defective, you have to send it all the way back to Palookaville.

The best place to buy products that are hard to hook up or install is at the local computer store because the clerks in the store will often do the installation work for you. If a problem comes up after you take the product home, you can call the store and get advice about how to solve the problem. Buy super-charged, ultra-fancy **PCs** locally, too, since configuring that kind of equipment can be difficult and often requires heaps of good advice.

Male Connector ❖ Female Connector

Math Coprocessor

You probably don't need to know about this. But I'll give you the bird's-eye view since you've looked up this entry. Math coprocessors perform floating-point calculations fast—much faster than your regular old **microprocessor** can. For this reason, people who use their computers to do lots of floating-point math sometimes add math coprocessors to their computers.

Before you run out and buy a math coprocessor to improve your PC's speed, however, I need to tell you a couple of things. First, many microprocessors already have math coprocessors built into them. For example, all of the 80486 microprocessors whose names include DX or DX2 have built-in math coprocessors. And so do Pentium microprocessors.

But there's something else you should know. Although floating-point calculations are usually just calculations that use numbers with decimal values (1.23 * 4.5678, for example), most **applications** don't actually do much floating-point math. Basically, applications that work with numbers that have decimals use tricks to turn num-bers-with-decimals into numbers-without-decimals—just so they don't have to do floating-point math. For example, an application can multiply all the values by 10,000. So instead of multiplying 1.23 by 4.5678, it multiplies 12,300 by 45,678 and then divides the result by 10,000.

The bottom line in all of this is that you probably don't need a math coprocessor. If you're looking to speed up your computer, your best bet is usually just to add more **memory.**

.·. **CPU**

Megabyte (MB) .·. **Byte**

Megahertz (MHz) .·. **Hertz (Hz)**

Memory

Memory is like the top of your desk. It's the temporary storage area your PC uses while it's working on tasks—just as your desktop is probably a temporary storage area you use when you work. When you start an **application,** for example, it's stored in memory. And any **files** you open are also stored in memory. The one thing you need to remember about memory is that whatever is stored in memory is lost when you turn off your PC.

In contrast, **floppy disks, hard disks,** and **CD-ROM** discs are permanent storage areas. Whatever is stored on them doesn't go away when your PC is turned off.

continues

Memory *(continued)*

Let me tell you a bit more about memory. First and foremost, **Windows 95** just loves memory. You need at least 4 **megabytes** (**MB**) of memory to run Windows 95, but the more memory your PC has, the faster Windows 95 will run. Having 8 MB is an improvement, for example. But throw 12 or 16 MB into your PC, and it will scream.

Most computers come with at least 4 MB of memory. But you can buy **expansion boards**—often called SIMMS—that add memory to a PC. Adding memory to a PC isn't difficult. If you've ever successfully assembled a child's toy on Christmas morning, you have the necessary skills. You can do it. Just make sure that you get instructions from the person who sells you the memory.

Oh, another thing. People who like acronyms use the term "RAM" to refer to memory. RAM is the shorthand name for random access memory. Advertisements for computers often tell you how much RAM a computer has because that term makes the computer sound cooler. (Or something.)

A little digression

Andrei Codrescu, the humorist heard on National Public Radio and the editor of *Exquisite Corpse* (a superb magazine), has suggested that computer memory is mined from the brains of humans and that whenever you buy more memory for your computer you are making someone more forgetful. Could this macabre idea be true? Since the advent of the personal computer, I *have* noticed that more people are misplacing their pocketbooks and leaving home without their house keys. . . .

 Cache Memory; Virtual Memory

Menu   All computer applications have menus with commands on them. To give a command, you first "open" the menu that contains the command. Then you choose the command.

To open a menu, you can either click it or press the Alt key and the letter that is underlined in the menu name. For example, to open the Programs menu in **Windows 95,** you can either click Programs or press Alt+P.

Once the menu is open, you can choose a command by using one of these methods:

Click the command name.

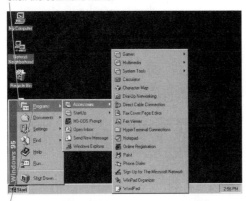

Press Alt and the underlined letter in the command name at the same time.

Press the ↑ or ↓ key until the command you want is highlighted, and then press Enter.

Dialog Box; Submenu

Microprocessor ⁖ CPU

Microsoft Network The Microsoft Network is Microsoft's
online service. With Windows 95 and a modem, you can
connect to The Microsoft Network.

Modem A modem—the word means modulator/demodulator—
is a hardware **device** for sending **files** and messages over
the telephone lines. To send a file or message, the modem
converts computer data to sounds and then sends the
sounds over the telephone lines to another modem and
computer at the other end of the telephone lines. To receive a file or message, the modem hears the sounds coming over the telephone lines and then converts the sounds
back to digital code that a computer can read.

This is my external
modem. It sits on my
desk next to my
computer. There's a little
on-off switch on the
back.

How fast a modem can send or receive data is measured
in bits per second, or bps. Modems that have higher bps
rates can send and receive data faster. When you are
shopping for a modem, buy a 28.8 Kbps model. They cost
more, but you'll save money in the long run because you
won't spend as much time when you use **online services,**
which charge by the hour. Fast modems can **download**
information more quickly.

 Baud; Fax/Modem; Internet

Monitor The monitor is the thing you stare at. It is also called the "screen" or the "display." While most monitors can display 25 rows and 80 columns of text—the equivalent of about half a page—monitors come in different sizes. If you read computer advertisements, you'll see 14-inch monitors, 15-inch monitors, and 17-inch monitors. The bigger the monitor, the more expensive. But a larger monitor can really reduce your eye strain, especially if you spend hours a day looking at the darn thing. (There's also such a thing as a "portrait" monitor, which displays the equivalent of an entire page.)

A monitor's size is measured as the distance between the opposite corners of the picture tube.

If you want to buy a monitor and money is no concern, get a noninterlaced, **Super VGA** monitor with a **dot pitch** of .28 mm and a **refresh rate** of 72 MHz or better. You may also want to get a larger monitor than the usual 14-inch size—perhaps 15 or 17 inches, for example. If money is a concern (and to be honest, when isn't it?), just make sure you try out the monitor before you plunk down your money to be certain that the screen is legible and that you don't see something annoying—like a noticeable flicker.

Preventing burn in

Keeping a monitor on too long with the same image on the screen can cause "burn in," a ghost-like image on the screen that won't go away because the image has eaten into the screen's interior phosphorous lining. To prevent burn in, turn off your monitor when you're not using it, or turn on one of the Windows 95 screen savers.

> **Display Adapter; ELF Radiation; Ergonomics; Interlacing; Pixel; Resolution**

Monochrome "Monochrome," as all Greek scholars and KayPro users know, means "one color." People usually use the term monochrome to describe **monitors.** Monochrome monitors do not display colors but instead present text and graphics in shades of a color. If a monochrome monitor displays everything in green, for example, everything shows up in different shades of green. Many laptop monitors are monochrome. But most desktop computers nowadays come with color monitors.

Motherboard The motherboard is the mother of all **boards.** If you lifted the case off the system unit and peered inside, you would see a motherboard similar to the one in the photo. The motherboard is the main circuit board to which cling the **CPU,** the ROM **chips,** all **expansion boards,** and the computer's memory chips.

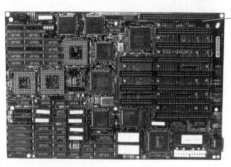

This is a motherboard.

:•. **Daughterboard**

Mouse A mouse is a pointing **device** for moving the cursor on the screen. By clicking, double-clicking, and dragging the mouse, you can choose **commands,** highlight text, move **objects,** and do many other tasks.

This is a mouse, of course.

The mouse has 2 buttons, 1 on the left and 1 on the right. Instructions in computer **applications** call for users to **click** or **double-click** the left or right mouse button. Sometimes clicking these buttons is called "left-clicking" and "right-clicking."

Be sure to have a mouse pad to roll your mouse across. A mouse pad gives the mouse traction and makes working with the mouse easier. At some point, however, crud and gunk particles from the mouse pad will collect around the little ball inside the mouse, and the mouse won't roll very easily. When that happens, turn the mouse over and un-screw the ball holder underneath. Remove the mouse ball with a pair of tweezers, and pick the crud and gunk out of the mouse. Then replace the ball and screw the ball holder back into place. The mouse will work fine after that.

Customizing your mouse

You can control the click speed and the **drag** speed of a mouse in **Windows 95**. To do so, click the Start button, and then choose Set-tings and **Control Panel**. In Control Panel, double-click Mouse. In the Buttons tab, you can set the double-click speed. In the Motion tab, you can set the pointer speed; this is the speed at which the mouse rolls on the mouse pad.

 Port; Trackball

Moving Files ❖ **Files**

Moving Windows ❖ **Window**

MS-DOS MS-DOS stands for Microsoft Disk Operating System. Sometimes it is called simply "DOS" (the word rhymes with "boss"). MS-DOS is a "text-based" **operating system** in which users type **commands** from the **keyboard** instead of clicking **objects** to start **applications.** With the **Windows 95** operating system, you no longer need MS-DOS, but you can still run MS-DOS applications in Windows 95.

> ❖ **DOS; MS-DOS Prompt; Starting Windows-Based Applications**

MS-DOS Prompt The MS-DOS Prompt command starts a session of MS-DOS. You might choose this command if you want to start an MS-DOS **application** in **Windows 95.** Specifically, you follow these steps to start an MS-DOS application using the MS-DOS Prompt command:

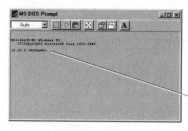

1 Click the Start button, and then choose Programs and MS-DOS Prompt. Windows 95 displays the MS-DOS **window.**

2 Type the commands at the prompt.

3 Type exit at the MS-DOS prompt when you want to end the MS-DOS session.

❖ **MS-DOS**

MSN ❖ Microsoft Network

Multimedia "Multimedia" is a one of the buzzwords people throw around a lot these days. Technically, multimedia really means that a product uses multiple mediums for communication. A new Tony Bennett CD, for example, uses one communication medium—music—while a book on music uses another communication medium—text in the form of ink on paper. If you combine the music with the text, you have multiple mediums—a.k.a., multimedia.

Practically speaking, what people mean when they refer to multimedia is compact discs, or CDs, that use multiple mediums for communication: text, music (and other sound), animation, video, and anything else the multimedia author can talk the multimedia publisher into.

To run a multimedia **application,** you need a powerful computer capable of producing high-quality sound and high-speed animation and video. This means you need a **sound card,** speakers, and, usually, a **CD player** (since multimedia applications usually come on CD-ROM discs).

Multitasking Multitasking is when a computer does more than 1 task at a time. For example, if your computer is printing a **file,** showing you a computer **game,** and formatting a **document** all at the same time, it is multitasking.

Not all **operating systems** are capable of multitasking. Some pretend at multitasking by letting you start and stop different **applications** at lightning speed. Instead of running 2 applications at once, you are actually stopping one and starting the other, but you do it so fast that you get the appearance of multitasking. **Windows 95** and OS/2 are true multitasking operating systems.

When you are multitasking, applications that are not on the screen are said to be "running in the background."

❖ **Switching Tasks**

Naming Files ❖ Files

Network A network is a collection of computers that are linked together for the purpose of sharing information. These days, most companies of any size have a network so that employees can trade **files**, messages, and gossip.

Besides sharing information, one of the chief benefits of having a network is being able to share **printers** and other peripheral **devices**—devices like monster **hard disks** and tape drives. Instead of having one printer for each employee, companies can have employees send their files to a single printer down the hall. That arrangement saves money on printers. Employees can also send faxes on a single **fax/modem** connected to a network. On most networks, you can even run **applications** that aren't on your **PC** but are on PCs elsewhere on the network.

Setting up a network, running all the **cables** together, and making all the computers work in sync is a difficult job that's best left to the system administrator, the person whose job it is to manage the network. Make use of this individual. If you have a problem, or if you're a beginner who's just learning to use a network, the system administrator can be a great resource.

Notebook ❖ Laptop

Numeric Keys The numeric keys are located on the right side of the **keyboard.** Once you've pressed the Num Lock key, you can use the numeric keys as you would the keys on a calculator.

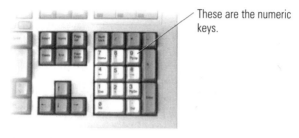

These are the numeric keys.

⁘ **Toggle Key**

Object The term "object" gets bandied about quite a bit and therefore has lost some of its meaning. In drawing **applications,** objects are the lines and shapes users draw. In some database applications, objects are the building blocks that make up databases. In programming, the term "object" refers to items that applications manipulate.

In **Windows 95,** "object" is used like the term "icon"—to mean the items you see on the desktop. The term also refers to OLE objects, which are parts of the **documents** that you can copy or move between applications.

⁘ **Icon; OLE**

OLE

OLE lets you share stuff between **documents.** Oh, sure, "stuff" doesn't sound like a very precise term. But it's tough to be precise about what you can do with OLE because OLE lets you share just about anything. Let me explain.

You use OLE to create what's called a "compound document"—a document **file** that combines 2 or more types of documents. For example, you might want to create a compound document that includes a long report written in Microsoft Word. On page 27 of your report, however, you might want to include a worksheet (or a worksheet fragment) created in Lotus 1-2-3. And on page 37 of your report, you might want to include a chart created in Microsoft Excel.

You could add other sorts of **objects**—such as recorded sounds. So your compound document would really consist of stuff created in different **applications** and pasted together into 1 big, compound document.

Using OLE to Create Compound Documents

To do all this pasting together and combining, you can often use an application's Edit Copy and Edit Paste (or Edit Paste Special) **commands.** Microsoft applications such as Word and Excel also include an Insert Object command that lets you add and create objects for a compound document. You indicate whether you want an object linked or embedded when you use the Edit Paste, Edit Paste Special, or Insert Object command. (See the next section.)

Distinguishing Between Linked Objects and Embedded Objects

A linked object—such as an Excel worksheet that you've pasted into a word processor document—gets updated whenever the source document changes. An embedded object doesn't. (You can, however, double-click an embedded object to open the application that created the embedded object and make your changes.)

What you absolutely need to know about OLE

Perhaps the most important tidbit for you to know about OLE is that it's easy to use. You don't have to do anything other than copy and paste the items—called "objects"—that you want to plop into the compound document. If you're working with applications that support the newest version of OLE, you may also be able to drag-and-drop objects between application **windows.**

Drag

Online Services An online service is a huge private computer **network.** Members can dial the service by using their **modems** and get reference information. They can also send **files** to other members and to users of the **Internet.** Online services charge either a monthly fee or a per-hour rate to customers.

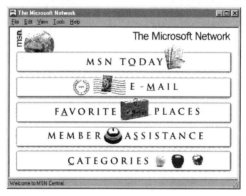

Most online services offer basic information such as daily news, stock quotes, and weather forecasts. Here you can see the basic services that The Miccrosoft Network offers. Online services also offer encyclopedias, dictionaries, and pharma-copoeias that members can use as references. On some services, you can even book travel reservations and shop.

continues

Online Services *(continued)*

All services offer hundreds of forums for their members. A forum is an online location where you can go to get information on a particular topic and to trade opinions with others who share your interests. There are forums for every topic under the sun, from dog grooming to UFO sightings.

America Online, CompuServe, GEnie, The **Microsoft Network,** and Prodigy are examples of online services.

A cost-saving tip

The cost of sending files over an online service can add up. You are usually billed whenever you send a file, but you can cut costs by using a **shareware** application called PKZIP. This application compresses files. Once a file has been "zipped," it is only about half its original size. Sending the compressed file takes half the time and cuts e-mailing costs in half. You can get PKZIP and its companion application PKUNZIP, which "unzips" files and returns them to their original size, by calling PKWARE at (414) 354-8699.

 Internet

Opening Applications Starting Windows-Based Applications

Opening Files Files

Operating System
An operating system manages your computer's **hardware,** such as the **memory,** the **CPU,** the **disks,** and any computer **peripherals. Applications** run on top of an operating system and use the operating system to avoid having to talk directly to the hardware.

This book assumes that the operating system your **PC** uses is **Windows 95.** But it's possible your PC uses another operating system, such as **MS-DOS, OS/2,** or even **UNIX.**

Option Buttons

Option buttons are sets of mutually exclusive choices. Sometimes option buttons are called "radio buttons."

You can easily identify an option button set because it's a group of round buttons with a border. This is the **dialog box** that WordPad displays when you choose the View Options **command.** The dialog box uses the Word Wrap set of option buttons to ask whether you want WordPad's word wrap feature turned on.

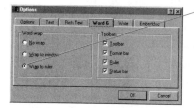

The selected option button shows a dot—called a "bullet"—in its center.

To select one of the option buttons in a set, you click the button.

You can also use the **keyboard** to select an option button. For example, you can use the Tab key to select an option button, and then press Enter. Or you can press the Up and Down arrow keys to select an option button, and then press Enter. Or if the option buttons in a set show underlined letters, you can press the Alt key and the underlined letter to select an option button. For example, you can select the No Wrap option button in the preceding dialog box by pressing Alt+N.

OS/2

OS/2 is another **operating system,** roughly akin to **Windows 95.** Like Windows 95, OS/2 can run several **applications** at once—including applications designed for **MS-DOS** or for versions of Windows earlier than Windows 95. This book, however, doesn't describe how to work with OS/2, although any of the material you read about **hardware** and **software** here still applies to PCs that run OS/2.

.·. **Operating System**

Parallel Port   A parallel **port** is a socket you use to connect a
parallel **device** to your computer. Most **printers** are
plugged into the parallel port. If your PC has more than
1 parallel port, the ports are labeled "LPT1" and "LPT2."
Just for the record, you probably need only 1 of these
ports if you plan to print using only a single printer.

PC   PC stands for "personal computer." (It also stands for
"politically correct," but that's another story.) Although
Apple Macintoshes are also PCs, the term always refers to
IBM and **IBM compatible computers.** Macintosh computers are often called "Macs."

The term "personal computer" was coined in the 1970s to
distinguish bulky mainframe computers from the smaller,
friendlier models that had just appeared on the scene.

Pentium   As I write this, Pentium is the name of the newest and
fastest processor **chip** made by Intel. It is the latest in the
Intel line, after the 80286, the 80386, and the 80486 chip.
(Intel has announced a successor to the Pentium, however. And that chip should be available by the time you
read this.)

When people say their computer is a 486, they mean it
has an Intel 80486 processor. Likewise with Pentiums.
If your parrot says it has a Pentium, that means it has—
or more likely you have—a computer with a Pentium
microprocessor.

   Bleeding-Edge Technology

Peripherals   A peripheral is a **device** that's connected to a PC to
make the PC more useful or more fun. For example, a
printer is a peripheral. So is a **joystick**, a **fax/modem**, a
modem, a **CD-ROM** drive, and a tape drive. To use some
peripherals, you have to install **expansion boards.**

Personal Finance Software

Personal finance software is **software** that's designed to help track finances and achieve financial goals.

You can record checks and balance your checkbook using personal finance software, as well as track investments such as stocks and bonds, real estate, and mutual funds. You can also use personal finance software for financial planning. For example, if you wanted to buy a house, you could use the software to devise a savings plan. Personal finance software also has chart features. For example, you can see a chart that shows your monthly income over the past year. The best known personal finance **application** is Quicken.

In Quicken, you fill in **windows** that resemble the pieces of paper you now fill in with a pen or pencil.

There is also such a thing as tax-preparation software, which is designed to do just that—help prepare your taxes. The great advantage of tax-preparation software is that it does all mathematical calculations for you. So no more punching calculator keys in the wee hours of the morn on April 15. All the tax forms are included with the software. TaxCut and TurboTax are 2 well known tax-preparation applications.

Personal Information Managers (PIMs)

Personal information manager applications (PIMs) help you organize your life. Most include an address book, a calendar, a scheduler, and a place for jotting down notes. The good ones have special features like the ability to print labels from address lists and the ability to search for information.

When you shop for a PIM, look for one that allows you to move information between "modules" rather than having to re-enter it. It's a bother to have to re-enter a client's name and address in the scheduler module, for example, when the client is already listed in the address book. Your PIM should also let you organize data as you see fit. For example, if you want to create a **directory** called "People to Borrow Money From," you should be able to do so.

Info Select, Lotus Organizer, and Okna Desktop Set are some of the personal information managers.

Pixel

On a **monitor** screen, images are composed of thousands of little dots called "pixels." The word "pixel" stands for "picture element."

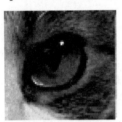

In this illustration, the cat's eye is composed of hundreds of pixels of various shades of gray and black.

The more pixels on a monitor screen, the better the image **resolution.** Monitors all tell you what their screen resolutions are by using numbers like 800-by-600 or 640-by-480. The first number is the number of horizontal pixels, and the second number is the number of vertical pixels.

:·. **Bit-Mapped**

Port   A port is a place where data is passed in and out of a
computer. A computer can have several ports, all found
along the back panel. There are ports for plugging in a
keyboard, for plugging in a **monitor,** and for plugging in
a **mouse.** Computers also have **parallel ports** and **serial
ports.**

This socket is a port.

PostScript   PostScript is a page-description computer language.
The language gives directions for scaling, or resizing,
fonts, for laying out pages, and for drawing lines and
shapes.

PostScript fonts are drawn using the PostScript language.
As such, they can be scaled to any type size. They are
known for their smoothness and are preferred by desktop
publishers because they conform to the high standards of
the typographic industry. Unlike bit-mapped fonts,
PostScript fonts are composed of lines and curves, so they
are easy for a computer to scale.

To use PostScript fonts, you must have a PostScript
compatible **printer.**

🐾 **Bit-Mapped; TrueType Fonts**

Power Cord The power cord connects a computer to a wall socket. It plugs into the back of the system unit. Before you plug a power cord into your wall socket, be sure your computer is turned off. You shouldn't have to pay for a power cord. It should come free with your PC.

Let's clear up some possible confusion

Power cords are not to be confused with "power chords," the ear-splitting guitar sounds made by heavy-metal musicians for the amusement of their deaf fans.

Power Strip A power strip is an electrical gizmo that has 6 to 8 electrical sockets on it. Make that 6 to 8 three-pronged sockets. Computers and computer devices need three-pronged, grounded sockets.

Here's my power strip.

If you have a **modem, printer, scanner,** or fax machine, you need a power strip to plug all that stuff in to. Using one of those octopus-like deals that turns 1 socket into 3 or 4 is not recommended since it's easy to knock it off the wall. You can buy a power director, which is a power strip that has an on/off switch. When you turn it on, you simultaneously turn on all the devices it's connected to.

A tip for when you buy a power strip

Buy a power strip that has a noise filter. It doesn't cost much more, and it's worth it because it filters out noise in the power lines and thereby gives computers cleaner power.

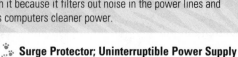 **Surge Protector; Uninterruptible Power Supply**

Presentation Applications

You use presentation applications to make tables, graphics, and charts and present them at seminars and business meetings. You can create transparencies, slides, and overhead projections using these applications. With some presentation applications, you can even produce video and animation.

The first slide in a PowerPoint presentation that I routinely show my wife.

If you're in the market for a presentation application, get one that's easy to use. Nothing spoils a presentation faster than watching the presenter fumble with the **software** and equipment. Get a presentation application that works with common graphics formats so that you can import graphics easily. The application should also have templates, which are preformatted screens that have borders and background color. If you think it would be useful, get an application that lets you copy presentations to **disk.** That way, you can distribute on-disk copies of your presentations to clients and customers.

Harvard Graphics and Microsoft PowerPoint are the 2 most popular presentation applications.

Printers

"Can I have that in writing?" people sometimes ask. As far as computers go, you can't have anything in writing until you print it. Images on a computer screen, Valentine letters, and financial records are mere abstractions until they're run through a printer and printed. So be sure to leave room in your computer-buying budget for a printer.

continues

Printers *(continued)*

There are 4 types of printers: **daisy-wheel printers, dot-matrix printers, ink-jet printers,** and **laser printers.** A home PC user will do just fine with a good dot-matrix or ink-jet printer. A business, however, will probably want to go with a laser printer. (If you plan to do a lot of printing, you'll find that a laser printer actually costs less per page than an ink-jet printer.)

You do have a choice to make when you choose an ink-jet or laser printer. You need to choose which language the printer speaks: **PostScript** or PCL. **Resolution** is higher on a PostScript printer, but a PostScript printer costs more. Unless you're doing **desktop publishing** or printing sophisticated graphics, you don't need the more expensive PostScript printer. You're fine with a PCL printer.

Connecting a printer

Most printers are connected to the system unit through the **parallel port,** but some printers use the **serial port.** These printers are called "serial printers." Serial printers are a hassle to work with, and if you buy one you may have to hire someone to get it to work on your system.

> ⁘ **Bit-Mapped; Fonts**

Printing Files ⁘ Files

Processors ⁘ CPU; Math Coprocessor

Prodigy ⁘ Online Services

Product Reviews At a magazine office, the sales department and the editorial department are often at war. The sales department would like to devote more pages to advertising. The editorial department would like to devote more pages to articles. If the sales department had its way, the magazine's sole purpose would be to print nice comments about the products advertised on its pages. That would make selling ads much, much easier. If the editorial department had its way, the colorful advertisements that debauch the pages of the magazine would be banished. That would give editors complete control over the magazine's appearance.

Who is winning this war between sales and editorial? Why, the sales department, of course!

In computer magazines, the unwritten rule is to never print anything bad about a product that is advertised on the pages of the magazine. In fact, if you see a headline on the cover of a computer magazine that reads "Printers: The Complete Lowdown," you can bet that the magazine is chock full of advertisements for **printers**. The product reviews are secondary. The idea to review printers that month probably originated with the employees in the sales department, who reasoned that they could sell more printer ads if they devoted an entire issue to printers.

When you read product reviews in computer magazines, keep a salt shaker handy. Everything should be taken not with one grain of salt but with several hundred. It's called a "conflict of interest" when the mayor awards a huge city contract to a nephew. But when a company takes out a 6-page glossy advertising supplement in a computer magazine and the magazine gives the company's products a glowing review, that's called "business as usual."

Programs ∴ **Applications**

Queue Jockey Radio stations use disk jockeys. The disk jockeys play the music. And they provide an endless stream of light banter. If you call some software publishers' technical support number, you'll hear a similar person: the queue jockey, or "QJ." While you're on hold, waiting for a technical support person, the QJ plays music and does a little talking. Usually, the QJ also tells you how many people are waiting in each of the technical support queues, or lines. As corny as this all sounds, I like QJs. I think they give you a sense of progress, a sense that you're moving forward in the line.

Quitting Applications ❖ Stopping Windows- Based Applications

Quitting Windows 95 ❖ Windows 95

QWERTY Pronounced "kwirty," this is the name of the standard **keyboard** found on most typewriters and with most computers. If you're wondering how a keyboard got such a silly name, look at the 5 keys to the right of the Tab key. Those keys are Q, W, E, R, T, and Y.

The QWERTY name is used to distinguish the QWERTY keyboard from the Dvorak keyboard.

The Dvorak keyboard is supposed to make typing easier in the same way that speaking Esperanto is supposed to make communication easier. I wonder which there are more of—Esperanto speakers or Dvorak keyboard users? I wonder if any Esperanto speakers use the Dvorak keyboard.

Radiation ⁙ ELF Radiation

Refresh Rate
This is the rate at which images form on the screen. On noninterlaced **monitors**, the refresh rate hovers at around 60 **hertz (Hz)**, or 60 times per second. On interlaced monitors, it's about 30 Hz. You can guess as much, but a higher refresh rate is usually better. The screen flickers less.

⁙ **Interlacing**

Renaming Files ⁙ Files

Renaming Folders ⁙ Folder

Repetitive Strain Injury ⁙ Ergonomics

Reset Button
Some computers have a Reset button on the front panel of the system unit. If your computer "hangs"— that is, if it does nothing no matter how frantically you press keys or move the **mouse**—you can press the Reset button. The computer will shut down and start up again.

Press the Reset button only as a last resort. When you press it, you lose any work you haven't saved. And you can damage data on your **hard disk** by pressing Reset. However, pressing Reset is easier on your computer than turning the power off and on again to restart it.

Resizing Windows ⁙ Window

Resolution

The word "resolution" is used to describe how clearly images and letters appear on a monitor screen. It also describes how clearly images and text appear on the printed page.

The resolution of a monitor screen is measured in **pixels.** For example, a VGA graphics monitor is 640 by 480 pixels, or simply 640x480, which means that it displays 640 horizontal pixels and 480 vertical pixels. The more pixels, the higher the screen resolution and the better the picture.

Instead of pixels, printer resolution is measured in dots per inch (dpi). Dots per inch is the number of dots a **printer** is capable of displaying in 1 square inch. **Laser printers** have the highest resolution, at 300 to 600 dpi. Low-quality **dot-matrix printers** have a resolution of 125 dpi.

∴ **Monitor**

Restoring Files ∴ Backing Up

Running Applications ∴ Starting Windows-Based Applications

Saving Files ∴ Files

Scanner

A scanner turns pages of text or pictures into files. It essentially takes a photograph of a page and turns that photograph into a file. Once you've got a file, you can noodle around with it using any number of **graphics applications.**

Scanners work by passing a light-sensitive element back and forth across the page, translating the colors it sees into **bits** that the computer understands. As you might have guessed, the quality of the scanned image depends on the quality of the scanner.

Screen Saver Burn in can result if a **monitor** is left on too long with the same image on the screen. The image eats into the phosphorous lining inside the screen, and you are left with a ghost-like image on the screen that won't go away. To avoid burn in, turn off your monitor when you're not using it, or get a screen saver. A screen saver comes on automatically when the computer has been left idle too long.

To use one of **Windows 95's** screen savers:

1 Click the Start button, and then choose Settings and Control Panel.

2 Double-click the Display **icon**. Windows 95 displays the Display Properties **dialog box**.

3 Click the Screen Saver tab.

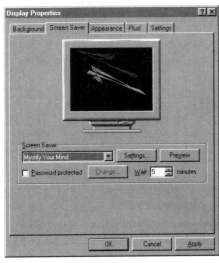

4 Click the down arrow for the Screen Saver drop-down list, and play around with the different screen savers until you find one you like.

5 Click OK.

The "Flying Windows" screen saver is a little frightening since it looks as though people are throwing things at you, and "Scrolling Marquee" (which displays the words "Windows 95 Is Cool" over and over again) was included at the suggestion of Beavis and Butthead, 2 low-level Microsoft Corporation programmers. Personally, I like "Starfield Simulation."

 Wallpaper

Scroll Bar Many **windows** have a vertical scroll bar along the right side of the screen. Some windows also have a horizontal scroll bar across the bottom. By manipulating the vertical scroll bar, you can move toward the beginning or toward the end of a **file.** By manipulating the horizontal scroll bar, you can move from side to side on the "page" in the file that appears on the screen.

Click above the scroll bar marker button to move backward in the file 1 screen at a time.

Click a scroll button to move—in the case of the vertical scroll bar—up or down 1 line at a time.

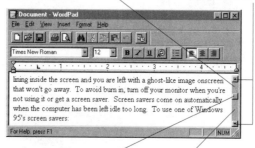

Click and drag the scroll bar marker button to move either forward or backward in a **document.**

Click below the scroll bar marker button to move forward in the file 1 screen at a time.

Learn from the scroll bar marker button

You can learn a couple of neat things by looking closely at the scroll bar marker button. First, you can learn how much of a document or list (or whatever) is displayed by looking at how big the scroll bar marker button is relative to the scroll bar. If the marker button is half the size of the scroll bar, you know that half of the list or document is displayed. The scroll bar marker button can also tell you where you are in a list or document. If the scroll bar marker button is near the top of the vertical scroll bar, for example, you're near the beginning.

Selection Cursor The selection cursor is the thing that marks the selected option in a **dialog box** or the selected text in a **text box.** OK. I know "thing" isn't a very specific noun. But how **Windows 95** marks an object using the selection cursor depends on the type of **object** being marked.

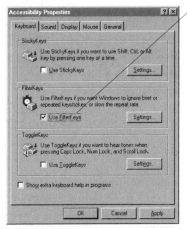

To mark a **check box** as selected, Windows 95 draws a line around the check box.

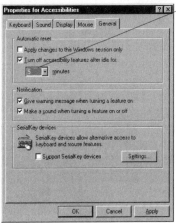

To mark a text box, **list box,** or **combo box's** contents as selected, Windows 95 highlights the text.

Serial Port A serial port connects hardware like a **mouse,** a **modem,** or an old **printer** to your computer. You need to be careful when you buy a serial **cable** to plug into a serial port because a serial port can have either a 9-pin or a 25-pin D connector. (D connectors get their name from their shape: They sort of look like a stretched-out letter "D".)

This is a cable for a 9-pin serial port. If you look carefully, you can actually count the 9 pins.

This is a cable for a 25-pin serial port. I don't expect you to count these pins.

Session A session is the period of time a user is at a computer terminal, between the time the computer is turned on and turned off. Not coincidentally, a session is also 1 visit to a psychiatrist's office.

Shareware Shareware is **software** that's given away free. If you like the software or intend to use it, you are supposed to send a small fee to the programmer who created it. Some shareware **applications** have code written into them that makes the applications inoperable unless users pay the fee within a certain period of time. Besides computer applications, clip art collections and font **files** are distributed as shareware. **Online services** and bulletin board systems are good places to look for shareware.

Freeware, a variation of shareware, is given away absolutely free. You don't have to send any money to the programmer who invented it, although most programmers ask for a postcard or some other acknowledgment. I guess they want to know who's using their software.

Software, shareware, and freeware aren't the only "wares"

Educational software is called "courseware." Promotional material distributed on CD-ROM discs is called "adware." When a company announces a software product but fails to come through with it, the product is called "vaporware." "Shovelware" results when a developer crams or "shovels in" a bunch of useless software onto a **disk** with the idea that quantity, not quality, attracts buyers.

Shortcut Icons Windows 95 lets you add shortcut **icons** for commonly used **documents, applications, folders,** and other items like these to the **desktop.** (The desktop is what you see on your **monitor** once Windows 95 is running.) Perhaps this doesn't seem like all that neat a deal, but it is. If these shortcut icons are displayed on the desktop, you can open a document, application, or folder simply by double-clicking its shortcut icon.

My Computer   Shortcut to Field Guide

This is a shortcut icon.

As part of the shortcut icon, Windows 95 uses another icon to identify the application that it'll instruct to open the document—in this case, the application is Microsoft Word.

Network Neighborhood

Recycle Bin

continues

Shortcut Icons *(continued)*

Creating a Shortcut Icon

To create a shortcut icon for a document, or file:

1 Start **Windows Explorer** by clicking the **Start button** and then choosing Programs and Windows Explorer.

2 Select the document that you want to create the shortcut icon for.

3 Choose the File Create Shortcut **command** so that Windows Explorer adds a shortcut icon to the folder.

4 Drag the shortcut icon to the desktop.

Shortcut Menu
Many Windows-based **applications** provide something called a "shortcut **menu**," or "context menu." Here's how this kind of menu works: Many applications are now smart enough to know which **commands** make sense in which situations. And many applications also know which commands you are most likely to use in those situations. If you want them to, these applications will display a shortcut menu that shows only these commands. All you need to do to display the shortcut menu is right-click the **mouse** on whatever **object** you want to manipulate.

Shutting Down
In **Windows 95,** shutting down is easy. Click the Start button, and then choose Shut Down. Windows 95 asks if you really want to shut down. Click Yes. (Once you've shut down Windows 95, you can turn off your computer's power.)

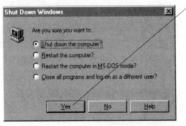

Once you choose Shut Down, Windows 95 displays this dialog box. Click Yes to finish shutting down.

 Turning Off Your Computer

Slots ❖ Expansion Slots

Software Software is the gray matter of the computer system. It tells the computer what to do. It also tells the **modem,** the **printer,** the **CD-ROM** drive, and other **peripherals** what to do. You can't get your hands on software. **Hardware,** on the other hand, goes "ping" when you tap it with a fingernail.

To use a musical metaphor, your stereo is hardware. So, I guess, are your records, any music CDs, and any tape cassettes. The music on those records, music CDs, and tape cassettes is like software. It provides, in essence, the instructions that your stereo needs to play music.

Sound Card A sound **card** is an **expansion board** that fits in the **motherboard** of the computer and allows the computer to play sound. Most **games** require sound cards. To enjoy sound, you ought to have speakers as well and, of course, **cables** to connect the speakers to your **PC.**

There are 2 sound card standards: Sound Blaster and AdLib. Most games use one or the other standard, so any sound card you get should be **compatible** with both.

Spreadsheet Applications

Spreadsheet **applications** do everything that an accountant's ledger does, only they do it far faster. You can use them for budgeting, bookkeeping, sales forecasting, or keeping track of personal finances.

Spreadsheets arrange information in rows and columns.

You enter text and numbers in the cells of a spreadsheet.

	January	February	March	Total	
Advertising	3990	570	890	5450	
Equipment	2330	3180	4080	9590	
Office	3840	3310	1770	8920	
Subcontractors	4300	1830	4320	10450	
Total	14460	8890	11060	34410	

Formulas use the values from cells to calculate totals, subtotals, averages, deviations, and more.

Most any spreadsheet application comes with functions for analyzing and quantifying data. The application makes the calculations for you. When you make a change to one of the numbers in the spreadsheet, the spreadsheet application automatically recalculates the sums and products. You can also make charts and graphs to tell at a glance what your finances look like.

The 3 "big-name" spreadsheet applications are Lotus 1-2-3, Microsoft Excel, and Quattro Pro.

Start Button

The Start button appears at the left end of the **Taskbar.** You use the Start button to start **applications,** to open **files,** to get to **Control Panel,** and even to exit from, or shut down, **Windows 95.** To press the Start button, you can click it. Or you can simultaneously press the Ctrl and Esc keys.

This, as you've no doubt guessed, is the Start button.

Starting Windows-Based Applications

You start a Windows-based **application** either by opening a **document,** or **file,** created by the application or by opening the application directly.

Starting an Application by Opening a Document

To start an application by opening a document:

1 Start **Windows Explorer** by clicking the **Start button** and then choosing Programs and Windows Explorer.

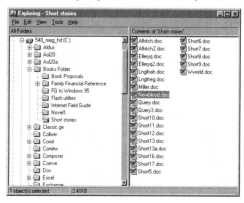

2 Display the **folder** that includes the document, or file.

3 Double-click the document, or file.

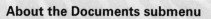

About the Documents submenu

Windows 95 has a Documents **submenu** that lists up to the last 15 documents you've used. If you see the document you want on this **menu,** you can open it by clicking it. To display the Documents submenu, click the Start button, and then choose Documents.

Starting an Application Directly

To start an application directly, without opening a document, or file:

1 Click the Start button, and then choose Programs.

2 Choose the submenu that names the application.

3 Choose the application from the submenu.

Stopping Windows-Based Applications
To stop an **application** in **Windows 95,** first save all the open **files** in the application. Then either choose the File Exit **command** or click the Close button, which is the button in the upper right corner of the screen that has an "X" in it. By the way, if you forget to save any open files before exiting, you'll see a message box that asks whether you want to save the files you're closing along with the application. Click Yes if you want to save the files.

❖ **Starting Windows-Based Applications**

Stripe Pitch
Most of the time, people calibrate the **resolution** of a **monitor** using **dot pitch** because the monitor uses dots of color to draw what's on the screen. Sometimes, however, the monitor draws stripes. When this is the case, predictably, people usually calibrate the resolution using stripe pitch instead of dot pitch. In general, the smaller the stripe pitch (or dot pitch, for that matter), the crisper the image.

Subfolder
I use the term "subfolder" to refer to a **folder** within a folder. This isn't some technical term I learned over at Microsoft, by the way. I just made it up.

Submenu
I use the term "submenu" to refer to a **menu** that appears when you choose another menu. This term I didn't make up. Computer trade book writers have used the term "submenu" ever since, well, ever since the first computer trade book writer crawled out of the primordial ooze.

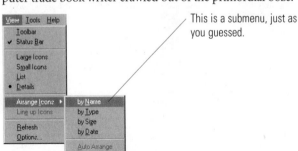

This is a submenu, just as you guessed.

Super VGA

"Super VGA" means that your **monitor** can display stuff at a pretty high **resolution.** The "VGA" part of the name stands for "Video Graphics Array." But you really don't need to remember any of this. Just make sure that the next monitor you buy is a Super VGA monitor.

Surge Protector

Computers want electricity to come at a steady rate. A split-second surge of power can damage a computer's central processing unit (**CPU**). It can also damage the **hard disk** and erase data. **Printers** and other peripheral **devices** don't like power surges, either.

To protect against power surges, you can get a surge protector. A surge protector provides an alternative path for electrical energy when it rises above the normal level on the power line. Surge protectors are also called "surge suppressers."

According to *Consumer Reports* magazine (November, 1994), you should get a model that meets the UL 1449 rating of 330 volts or better, although the magazine says to "steer clear of devices with a rating higher than 500 volts—that's unnecessarily high." The magazine adds, "A good surge suppresser should also have an internal fuse or circuit breaker that trips when the device ceases to protect." In the *Consumer Reports* tests, these models performed best: Trippite's Terminator ($50) and Command Console Plus ($95), the Surge Patrol 95004 ($50), the Titan Surge Defender Plus ($69), and the Panamax Supermax ($129).

Power Strip; Uninterruptible Power Supply

Switching Tasks

To switch tasks in **Windows 95,** use the **Taskbar.** The Taskbar is the bar along the bottom of the screen. It shows the Start button on its left side. To the right of the Start button are buttons that represent the **applications,** or programs, that are open.

To switch to an application that's open, click its window or taskbar button.

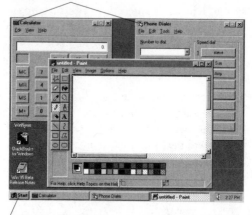

To open a new application, click the Start button. With Windows 95, you can run several applications at the same time.

You can have more than one **file** open in an application. To switch between open files, click the Window **menu,** and then click the name of the file you want to switch to.

 Multitasking

System Requirements

When you get or shop for a new piece of **software,** one of the first things you should do is see what its system requirements are. System requirements are the minimal requirements and optimal conditions for running the software. The system requirements might also include optional **devices** that make the software more useful.

Here is a typical list of system requirements:

Requirement	Description
Computer type	Whether the software requires an **IBM compatible computer** or a Macintosh.
Processor	What type of microprocessor, or **CPU**, is required. Some software does not run on ATs (80286 processors) and XTs (8086 or 8088 processors) and requires an 80386, 80486, or Pentium microprocessor.
Disk drive	The need for a 5¼-inch or a 3½-inch disk drive if the software comes on 5¼-inch or 3½-inch **disks**. Some software today even comes on a CD, so you need a CD drive to install it.
Disk space	How much disk space is needed for the application's **files**.
Memory	The minimal **memory** requirement.
Operating system	Whether the application runs in **Windows 95, DOS**, or **OS/2** or in some other **operating system**.

By the way, there's a little worksheet in the "Quick Reference" section of this book that lets you describe your system in detail. You might want to take a couple of minutes right now and fill it out. (To do this, you might need to find the original invoice or sales literature for your PC.) Knowing exactly what the parts of your PC system are will make it easier to think about system requirements.

System Unit   The system unit is the metal box that holds the **motherboard,** the power supply, your **disks,** and probably just about every other piece of **hardware** you've got connected to your computer—except the **monitor, mouse,** and **keyboard.**

Tab

In **Windows 95,** the term "tab" is used in a couple of ways. One way is to refer to the Tab key. Another way is to fit more options in a **dialog box.** If there's too much stuff to fit in a dialog box, Windows 95 and Windows-based **applications** separates options onto different "pages," each sprouting a "tab" that you can click to display that page.

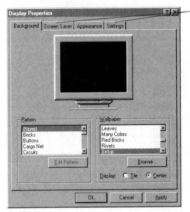

To move to a "page" of options, click the tab for that page.

Taskbar

The Taskbar shows at the very bottom of your screen. It provides the **Start button** and buttons for any additional **applications** that you or **Windows 95** have started.

You can use the Taskbar's **task buttons** to move another application to the foreground.

⁘ **Switching Tasks**

Task Buttons

Windows 95 shows a task button on the **Taskbar** for each **application** that you or Windows 95 starts. You can make an application the foreground application by clicking its task button.

I don't know what else to call these buttons, so I'm going with "task buttons."

Task Switching ❖ Switching Tasks

Tax Preparation Software ❖ Personal Finance Software

Technical Support Both **hardware** manufacturers and **software** developers offer help to their customers whenever they get stuck. This help is called "technical support." So if you've got a problem with that brand new **PC** you just bought, you can often get help by calling the manufacturer's technical support people. And if you can't figure out how to complete a task with the new release of a software **application,** you can call the software developer and get an answer.

I don't want to scare you, but technical support is more important than most people realize. If you have a problem with some hardware gizmo or with some piece of software, you need to be able to contact the people who produced the thing. For this reason, I probably wouldn't ever buy hardware or software from a company without first checking out its technical support. To do this, simply try calling them a few times. Can't get through? If you find it irritating now, think how frustrated you'll feel if you can't get in touch with them when you have a real problem. Yikes.

Oh, one final thing: In the "Quick Reference" section of this Field Guide, I've listed a bunch of technical support numbers for both hardware manufacturers and software developers. I thought it'd be handy for you to have these numbers all in one place. I will say, however, that these numbers change with some regularity. So you'll find yourself penciling in new numbers now and again. You'll also want to pencil in any numbers for hardware manufacturers and software developers that I didn't list but that you still need.

Text Box A text box is simply an input blank you fill in by typing. To do this, select the text box (such as by clicking it), and then start typing.

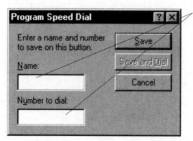

These input blanks, or boxes, are text boxes.

Deleting Characters in a Text Box

Position the insertion point by clicking or using the Left and Right arrow keys. Use the Backspace key to erase the character that precedes the insertion point; use the Del key to erase the character that follows the insertion point.

Replacing the Contents of a Text Box

Position the insertion point at the beginning of the text box by clicking. Drag the **mouse** to the last character of the text box to select the entire text box contents. Then type the replacement text. What you type replaces the selected text.

Toggle Key A toggle key is a on-off key. It works one way until you press it and then works the opposite way until you press it again. These are the 5 toggle keys on the **keyboard**:

Key	What it does
Caps Lock	When you press Caps Lock, ALL THE LETTERS YOU TYPE ARE UPPERCASE. WHEN YOU PRESS IT AGAIN, the letters return to lowercase.
Ins (Insert)	After you press Ins, the text you type on the screen covers, or overtypes, the text that is already there. Press it again to make the text you type push the text that is already there out of the way.
Num Lock	When you press Num Lock, the keys on the numeric keypad stop being cursor-movement keys and become calculator keys. They'll keep doing that until you press Num Lock again.
Pause	When information is gliding across the screen so quickly that you can't read it, press Pause. What's on the screen will lock in place until you press Pause again, at which time everything will go kittywumpus (that is, start gliding across the screen again). The Pause key is in the northeast corner of the keyboard.
Scroll Lock	This is supposed to be a toggle key, but it's really a nothing key. It doesn't do anything. If you turn off the lights and press this key up and down real fast, the Scroll Lock light in the upper right corner of the keyboard will wink at you.

Can't tell whether a toggle key is toggled?

If you can't tell whether a toggle key is in effect, look for any little lights in the upper right corner of the keyboard. If a toggle key is on, its light will be on, too.

 Numeric Keys

133

Trackball

A trackball is a stationary **mouse.** Instead of rolling it around on your desk, you turn it with your thumb. Like a mouse, trackballs have left and right buttons to click.

Trackballs are often found on laptop computers.

Three-handed users

The inventor of the mouse had 3 hands—2 to work the keyboard and 1 to manipulate the mouse. The trackball inventor had 3 hands, too. What can mere mortals with 2 hands do? After all, when you're working, it's hard to feel your way from the keyboard to the mouse and back all the time.

I have a suggestion: the soccer mouse. The soccer mouse is a sort of large trackball that lies on the floor under the desk. Users roll it around with their feet. Instead of clicking the soccer mouse, they bounce it once with their big toe. They bounce it twice to double-click.

TrueType Fonts

TrueType **fonts** are designed to look the same on the screen as they look when printed. Unlike bit-mapped fonts, TrueType fonts are composed of lines and curves, so they are easy for the computer to scale. **Windows 95** can generate TrueType fonts.

∴ **Bit-Mapped; PostScript**

Tube

Before transistors and integrated circuits, TVs and radios—and computers— had vacuum tubes like this one. The job of these tubes was to amplify signals from TV or radio stations when they arrived. However, tubes had to warm up before they could do anything. When you turned on a radio back in the old days, you had to wait a moment or two for the tubes to warm up and the sound to come on.

Once I saw a classic example of film noir strangeness called *Kiss Me Deadly* (1955) at the Roxie theater in San Francisco. In the movie, Ralph Meeker plays a sleazy gumshoe trying to ransom some radioactive material (called the "the great what's-it" in the movie). Whenever Meeker returned to his apartment, he loosened his tie, turned on the radio, and poured a scotch and soda. It always took a good minute or two for the sound on the radio to come on.

On the way out of the theater, I heard somebody ask, "What was with his radio? Why did it take so long for it to play?" The tubes had to warm up, that's why.

Turbo Button

Some computers have a Turbo button on the front panel of the system unit. You can press this button to make the computer work slower. Why would you want to do that? I think the idea is to make games work slower so that players can kill Martians more easily, but I'm really not sure. This button is an anachronism, sort of the **curb feeler** of computers.

Most computers have a Turbo light on the front panel. The Turbo light comes on whenever the computer is turned on.

Turning Off Your Computer
Never turn off a computer without first closing all **files,** or **documents,** and **applications.** If you just press the power switch and neglect to close files and applications beforehand you'll likely lose or corrupt files and damage the **hard disk.**

Should you turn off your computer?

Theologians are still arguing about whether you should press the power switch and turn off your computer when you finish using it or simply let it run all the time. The turn-it-off school says that you should turn a computer off at the end of the day. If you leave it on all the time, the fan and hard drive never get a rest, and they wear out faster. The let-it-run school maintains that turning a computer off and on makes the circuits cool down and heat up, and that makes them contract and expand, which makes them wear out faster.

Shutting Down

Turning On Your Computer
To turn on a computer, switch on the **monitor,** and then press the power switch. After a moment, you will see the **Windows 95** desktop.

Ever heard the term "boot?"

Turning on a computer is sometimes called "booting." That's because when you turn on a computer, it looks for instructions that tell it to go to more important instructions, and those instructions tell it to go to yet more important instructions, and then you arrive at the operating system **interface.** In this instance, the computer is doing what the poor are always being told to do: "pulling itself up by its bootstraps."

Reset Button

Typeface ⁘ Fonts

Typing Characters

To type characters and see them appear on the computer screen, place your hands just a little bit above the **keyboard,** and start wiggling your fingers.

These keys are especially useful for typing characters:

Key	What it does
Backspace	Erases characters to the left of the text cursor.
Caps Lock	Makes characters appear in uppercase. This is a **toggle key.** Press it a second time after you finish typing uppercase characters to type lowercase characters once again.
Ins (Insert)	Makes the characters you type cover up, or overtype, the characters that were already there. This is also a toggle key. Press it again to make the characters you type push the characters that are already there out of the way.
Shift	When pressed along with a letter key, makes a capital letter.
Tab	Moves the text cursor over 1 tab stop.

⁘ **Numeric Keys**

Undeleting

To undelete means to get back a **file** that you deleted. Undeleting is easy as pie in **Windows 95.**

Undeleting a File

To undelete a file:

1 Go to the **desktop,** if it isn't already showing. (To do this, click the Minimize button in the upper right corner of the **application** window. The Minimize button is the first of the 3 buttons that appear there; it has a line at the bottom—and not a square or " X.")

2 Double-click Recycle Bin.

Recycle Bin

3 Click the file you want to undelete. If you want to undelete more than 1 file, click it while holding down the Ctrl key.

4 Choose the File Restore **command.** Windows 95 puts the undeleted file back into its original **folder.**

Undo   Most computer **applications** have an Undo button or an Undo **command.** Undo "undoes" the most recent thing you did in the application. For example, if you accidentally erased Sharon Stone's telephone number or Matt Dillon's telephone number from a computer **file** and you needed to call her or him on Valentine's Day, you could press the Undo button to get the telephone number back. However, Undo can only undo your most recent action (or, in some applications, your most recent 2 or 3 actions). If you erased that telephone number and did 4 or 5 things afterwards, you'd be out of luck. You'd have to kiss Sharon Stone or Matt Dillon good-bye.

In Microsoft Office applications, the Edit menu's first command is always Undo.

Besides Undo, most applications also have a button or command called "Redo" (meaning "do again"). Redo is a handy command. It undoes your most recent "Undo" action.

Uninterruptible Power Supply   An uninterruptible power supply is a fancy electronic gadget that sends electricity to your computer if there is a power failure. These gadgets are not generators, however. Typically, they work for 10 or 15 minutes, ample time for you to save the **file** you're working on and turn off your computer.

⁘ **Power Strip; Surge Protector**

UNIX

The name UNIX sounds like "eunuchs." UNIX is a multitasking **operating system,** and it is also a *multiuser* operating system, meaning that it allows 2 or more people to use the same computer at the same time. Each person has his or her own **monitor** and **keyboard,** of course. But all these monitors and keyboards are connected to the same **system unit.** However, UNIX takes up a lot of disk space and is difficult for beginners to master.

Utility Software

Utility **software** is designed to diagnose and fix problems or help make your computer run more smoothly. There is utility software for fixing damaged **hard disks,** preventing computer **viruses,** and compressing **files.**

The most famous of the utilities is called Norton Utilities. This one can restore a damaged hard disk and help you recover deleted files. It also rearranges data on a hard disk so that all the data in each file is stored in roughly the same place. That makes it easier for the computer to access a file. Instead of having to jump around the disk to pull the various parts of the file together, the computer has to look in only 1 place, which speeds things up.

Anti-virus utilities protect against viruses. These applications know what virus files look like, and they can search for and destroy them on the hard disk.

Last but not least is compression software. This utility software compresses data files to make more room on your hard disk.

Free utilities

Windows 95 comes with a couple of handy utilities called DriveSpace and Backup. Choose Accessories from the Programs **menu,** and then choose System Tools and DriveSpace to use the DriveSpace utility, which compresses the files on a hard disk and makes more hard disk space available. Choose Accessories from the Programs menu, and then choose Microsoft Tools and Backup to use the Backup utility. Backup lets you back up a bunch of files at one time onto just about any kind of backup **device: floppy disks,** a tape, or another disk.

 Backing Up; Disk Compression

Video Adapter ⁘ Display Adapter

Virtual Memory "Virtual memory" simply refers to the disk space a computer uses as **memory**. I mention this here because **Windows 95** uses virtual memory. Fortunately, you don't have to do anything to get Windows 95 to do the virtual memory thing. Windows 95 takes care of the whole process all by itself.

Virtual Reality Virtual reality **applications** are supposed to make users think they're "really there." Users wear helmets, 3-D goggles, and gloves. Depending on how they move their hands inside the gloves, they hear and see different sounds and sights in an artificial environment. People usually say "Wow!" after they take off the helmet and gloves. Then they eat a pizza or a burger.

Virus A virus is a devious piece of computer code that looks innocuous but "infects" computers and either causes damage or does something annoying. For example, one famous virus erased all **files** created on April Fool's Day. That wasn't funny, especially for businesses that lost all their receipt records for that day. The infamous Michelangelo virus made the words "Happy Birthday" appear on computer screens on March 6, Michelangelo's birthday.

Viruses are spread in executable code (computer programs) and not in data files. You can get anti-virus **utility software** that checks for viruses on a **hard disk** and destroys them.

Just so you know, if you don't shamelessly share floppy disks and **applications** with other users, there's almost no way you can catch a virus. If you love to **download** files from bulletin board systems or if your kid trades **games** at school, however, you're almost certain to catch a virus in short order.

Virus trivia

Different kinds of viruses have special names. A "Trojan horse" is a virus disguised as a game or an application. This virus, like the Trojan horse itself, appears to be useful but does all kinds of damage in the background. A "worm" makes many, many copies of itself and eats up all the space on a hard disk.

Wallpaper   In computer land, "wallpaper" refers to the decorations that appear on the screen when you first turn on your computer and those that appear around the sides of the screen when the computer is in use. To change the wallpaper in **Windows 95,** click the Start button, and then choose Settings, and then **Control Panel.** Click Display, and click the Background tab, if necessary. On the right side of the screen, you can choose from a number of wallpaper types. "Egyptian Stone" looks awful, and "Leaves" is rather gaudy. I like "Sofia," myself. It's my daughter's name.

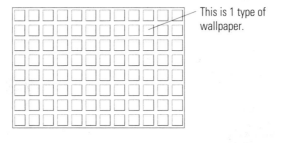

This is 1 type of wallpaper.

Wildcard Characters   Wildcard characters stand for other characters in an expression. For example, you might use wildcard characters as part of specifying the **file** name you enter in a **dialog box.** The most common wildcard characters are the ? and * symbols. A ? can stand for any single character. An * can stand for any single character or any group of characters.

Window

So important are windows in the Windows 95 operating environment that they named the **operating system** after them! Here are instructions for moving a window, resizing a window, and closing a window.

Moving a Window

To move a window, use the **mouse** to grasp the window by the title bar and drag it somewhere. The title bar is the strip of color at the top of the window; it shows the name of the **application** and the name of the **file**. As you drag the title bar, an outline of the window appears so that you can see where you're dragging the window. After you place the window where you want it, release the mouse button.

Resizing a Window

To "resize" a window means to change its size. The 3 buttons in the upper right corner of the window are the basic resizing tools. Here's how to use them:

Button	Name	What it does
▬	Minimize	This button shrinks the window down to nothing. Your file is still open after you click this button, even though you can't see the file. To open the window and see the file again, click the application name on the **Taskbar.** The Taskbar is the bar along the very bottom of the screen that shows the Start button on its left.
▣	Restore	Click this button to shrink the window by a third. Once you do that, the Maximize button replaces the Restore button.
☐	Maximize	Click this button to maximize the window so it fills the screen. Once you do that, the Restore button replaces the Maximize button.
✕	Close	Click this button when you want to close the application removing the window from the desktop.

Closing a Window

To close a window, click the Minimize button, which is the first of the 3 buttons that are displayed in the upper right corner of the window. When you want to open the window again, click the application name on the Taskbar, which appears along the bottom of the screen.

 Drag; Scroll Bar

Windows 95
Windows 95 is the name of an **operating system** put out by Microsoft Corporation. It is an upgrade to the older Windows system. With Windows 95, users can run more than 1 **application** at the same time, switch quickly between applications and **files,** and also move data rapidly between applications and files.

If Windows 95 is installed on your computer, it comes on automatically. You turn on your computer. Windows 95 starts.

 Multitasking

Windows Explorer
Windows Explorer lets you do 2 things: It lets you view and work with your computer's **disks** and the **files** you've got stored on your disks. And it lets you view and work with the other parts of your computer: its **fonts, Control Panel,** and **printers.**

continues

W

Windows Explorer *(continued)*

Starting Windows Explorer

To start Windows Explorer, click the Start button, and then choose
Programs and Windows Explorer.

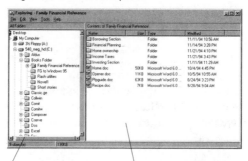

Windows Explorer uses a
folder pane to show the
folder structure.

Windows Explorer uses a file pane to
show the **subfolders** and the files in the
active folder. It provides information such
as the file size in **kilobytes (KB)** and the
date on which the file was last modified.

Selecting Disks

To select a disk, click the disk icon.

Selecting Folders

To select a **folder,** scroll through the folder pane until you see the
folder you want. Then click the folder.

If the folder is a subfolder in another folder (the "parent folder"), you
may need to first select the parent folder and then display its subfolder. You can do this by clicking the parent folder.

Windows Explorer alerts you to subfolders

Windows Explorer places a plus sign (+) in front of a folder's icon if that folder
has subfolders.

Selecting Files

To select a file in the active folder, scroll through the file pane until you see the file you want. Then click the file.

You can select multiple files by clicking the first file, holding down the Shift key, and then clicking the last file. Or you can hold down the Ctrl key and then click each file.

Understanding Windows Explorer's Different Icons

Windows Explorer uses different icons to represent folders and the various types of **documents,** or files. If you've come this far, you'll probably find it helpful to know what the different icons represent. Here's a list of the Windows Explorer icons:

Icon	Description
	Represents your **desktop.** If you click the desktop **icon,** Windows Explorer uses the file pane to show everything on your desktop—including any **shortcut icons.**
	Represents your computer, including its disks, printers, and any system folders for fonts and Control Panel settings. If you click the computer icon, Windows Explorer uses the file pane to show your computer's disks, printers, system files, and Control Panel.
	Represents a **floppy disk** drive. If you click the floppy disk drive icon, Windows Explorer uses the file pane to show the folders and files on the floppy disk.
	Represents a **hard disk** drive. If you click the hard disk drive icon, Windows Explorer uses the file pane to show the folders and files on the hard disk.
	Represents a folder. If the folder is active, the folder appears open. If the folder is inactive, the folder appears closed. If the folder holds subfolders, Windows Explorer places a plus sign (+) at the front of the folder.
	Represents an application file. You can start the application by double-clicking the application file icon or by selecting it and then choosing the File Open command. The application file icons look different depending on which application they're associated with.
	Represents an associated document file. You can start the associated application and open this document file by double-clicking it or by selecting it and then choosing the File Open command. The exact appearance of an associated document file icon depends on the application it's associated with. Notice that the application icon—in this example, for Microsoft Word—appears in the upper left corner of the icon.

continues

Windows Explorer *(continued)*

Icon	Description
	Represents an unassociated document file—that is, a document file that is not associated with an application. You can't open this document file by double-clicking. You can use the File Open With command to open this document file, but Windows Explorer asks you for the name of the application. To identify the application, you just select it from a list box of applications. (Windows Explorer changes the name of the command from File Open to File Open With if the selected document file isn't associated with an application.)
	Represents a **CD-ROM** drive. If you click the CD-ROM icon, Windows Explorer uses the file pane to show the folders and files that are on the CD.
	Represents your computer's fonts. If you click the fonts icon, Windows Explorer uses the file pane to show all the fonts installed on your computer.
	Represents Control Panel. If you click the Control Panel icon, Windows Explorer uses the file pane to show an icon for each of the Control Panel settings.
	Represents the printers available to your computer. If you click the printers icon, Windows Explorer uses the file pane to show an icon for each of the installed printers.
	Represents the **network** your computer is connected to. If you click the Network Neighborhood icon, Windows Explorer uses the file pane to show the other computers, disks, folders, and files that you can use because they're part of your network. (This works only if you *are* connected to a network.)
	Represents the Recycle Bin. If you click the Recycle Bin icon, Windows Explorer uses the file pane to show the files you've deleted. You can undelete files in the Recycle Bin.
	Represents another computer that your computer can access remotely—or vice versa. If you click the Dial-Up Networking icon, Windows 95 sets itself up for remote access.
	Represents your briefcase. If you click the My Briefcase icon, Windows 95 synchronizes the files in your briefcase by making sure your briefcase contains the most recent version of any file.

Word Processor The first word processors were little more than typewriters, but the word processor has evolved over the years to become a valuable writing tool. Using a word processor today, you can format text, change the type size and typestyle of letters, build tables, check your writing for spelling accuracy, lay out pages in different ways, move text from page to page, decorate pages with graphics, and include footnotes, end notes, and tables of contents. Some word processors have features found in desktop publishing **applications.**

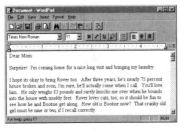

This is the WordPad application window.

WordPro, Microsoft Word, and WordPerfect are the 3 most popular word processors. But if you've got only light writing to do and are on a tight budget, you should know that **Windows 95** comes with a handy little word processor named WordPad.

 **Desktop Publishing**

WYSIWYG

WYSIWYG stands for "what you see is what you get." The word is pronounced "wizzy wig." WYSIWYG **fonts** and graphics appear on a computer screen exactly as they will look when they are printed. With a WYSIWYG **application,** you can play around with text and graphics on the screen and not have to worry that the **printer** will change the appearance of your work when it's transferred to paper.

For you history buffs

The term "WYSIWYG" was invented by Flip Wilson, a comedian who used to dress in drag on his early 1970s TV show and holler, "What you see is what you get, honey!"

Zulu Time

"Zulu Time" is a slang term for Greenwich mean time. Which brings up an idea I have. I'd like to read a seafaring novel that begins, "Guidry crossed the international date line in a schooner. Meantime, in Greenwich mean time, his brother Reginald..."

Windows 95 has a neat feature for seeing where all the time zones are, including Greenwich mean time. Click the Start button, and then choose Settings and Control Panel. In Control Panel, double-click the Date/Time tool, and then click the Time Zone tab. You'll see a map of the world. Click around the map to see the various time zones and their names.

TROUBLE-
SHOOTING

●●●

*Got a problem? Starting on the next page are
solutions to the problems that sometimes plague
new users of personal computers. You'll be on your
way and safely out of danger in no time.*

STARTING YOUR PERSONAL COMPUTER

Your Computer Won't Start

If you turn on your computer and it won't start at all—if you don't even hear the fan start whirling—you've got a power problem.

Check all the "On" switches

This is pretty obvious stuff, but make sure the system unit power switch is on. If you're using a **surge protector** or **power strip,** make sure that its power switch is on. (To make things tricky, some surge protectors have a reset button that needs to be reset if there has been a power surge or a sag in line strength.)

If you still can't even get power to the computer, try plugging something else into the same power outlet—such as a lamp—to see if it works. If the power outlet still doesn't work, check the fuse or circuit breaker for the outlet. But after that, it's time to call an electrician.

Oh, one other idea. When I first moved into my house, I inadvertently plugged my computer into a power outlet that could be turned on and off with a light switch. You know the kind of setup I mean—it's supposed to be used for table lamps. After I figured this out, I used the light switch as a kind of master power-strip switch. And it was kind of fun for a while. But it was also kind of dangerous. Friends and family would occasionally flip that switch thinking it was for the lights. Whenever this happened, I lost whatever work I hadn't already saved on **disk.**

Check the computer's power supply

If you're sure that your computer is getting power and that the power switch is on, and yet your computer still doesn't start, you know the problem is with the computer's power supply. This is something you'll need to have a repair technician fix.

You Get the "Press F1 to continue or F2 to access setup" Message

You get this message if your computer can't pass its power-on self test, or POST, successfully. That is, when your computer (with the help of the **BIOS**) ran through its test of itself, something didn't work quite right.

Press F1 to ignore the problem

If you've got work you absolutely have to get done, this isn't a bad approach. It's akin to starting your car, hearing some funny noise under the hood or from the rear axle, and then putting the car into gear and driving off anyway.

The problem with this approach, of course, is that ignoring the problem doesn't make it go away.

Press F2 if you've made a hardware change

When your PC runs through its power-on self test, it's checking to see whether its system configuration file—the description of your computer **hardware**—matches the actual hardware. In essence, the power-on self test asks questions like, "Says here that we've got 16 MB of memory—is that right?" Then it goes out and looks at how much memory you have.

The power-on self test makes a bunch of these checks: which disks you have, how much memory you have, whether you've got a math coprocessor, and so forth. If you've installed or changed some chunk of hardware, you can press F2 to access an application that lets you update the system configuration file so that it matches reality. To do this, you'll need to find the user guide that came with your computer. (It will provide you with instructions for using the setup application.) Or better yet, you can telephone the technical support number of the company that sold you the new hardware or the computer and ask the technical support folks for help. (Remember that the "Quick Reference" section of this Field Guide includes a list of the technical support numbers for a bunch of hardware manufacturers and software developers.)

continues

You Get the "Press F1 to continue or F2 to access setup" Message
(continued)

Take your computer to a repair shop

If you haven't made any changes to your computer hardware and your personal computer fails its power-on self test, it means 1 of 2 things. Maybe the system configuration file never did describe your computer correctly. (This is unlikely, however, unless you bought your PC from a manufacturer who has sloppy or zero quality control.) Or maybe some part of your computer has gone toes up. In this case, I think your best bet is to just take your computer back to wherever you bought it and ask for it to be checked out and repaired.

You Get the "Non-System disk or disk error" Message

When you turn on your PC, it thinks it's supposed to get the **operating system** from your A: **floppy disk** drive. So it looks there first. Ideally, your A: floppy disk drive is empty. In this case, your computer says to itself, "Well, gee, maybe I'd better check the hard disk drive." When your computer checks the hard disk drive, it finds the real operating system (probably **Windows 95** but possibly MS-DOS or even OS/2). Then your computer starts the operating system, and next thing you know you're on your merry way.

If, however, you've got a floppy disk in the A: floppy disk drive, your computer thinks it should be able to find the operating system on that disk. When it can't, it displays a message like this:

```
Non-system disk or disk error

Replace and press any key when ready
```

Remove the floppy disk from the A: floppy disk drive

To fix this error, just remove the offending floppy disk from the A: drive. Then press one of the keyboard's keys. It doesn't matter which key. You can press Enter, Esc, or anything else.

You Don't Start Windows 95

If you leave a system floppy disk—also known as a "bootable floppy disk"—in the A: floppy disk drive and turn on your computer, your computer reads the operating system from this floppy disk rather than from the hard disk. If this happens, you'll see the MS-DOS prompt on the screen instead of the Windows 95 desktop:

A:> ——————— This is what the MS-DOS prompt looks like.

Remove the floppy disk from the A: drive, and then reboot your computer

The easiest way to fix the perplexing problem of the wrong operating system or a partial operating system is just to remove the bootable floppy disk from the A: drive and then reboot your computer. To reboot, press Ctrl+Alt+Del.

Your Monitor Doesn't Display Anything

Suppose you turn on your PC and your **monitor.** Suppose you hear the thing start coming to life, but then nothing appears on the monitor. What should you do? I've got 3 ideas for you.

Make sure the monitor is on and connected

I'm kind of embarrassed to admit that I've had this problem before. But just getting power to a monitor can be tricky. Make sure the monitor power switch is on and also that whatever the monitor plugs into is on. And make sure the monitor's **cables** are all correctly connected.

Check the contrast

I tried to use a friend's computer the other day and couldn't get the monitor to work. What was the problem? It just so happens that, as a screen-saving technique, he turns down the brightness whenever he's not using the monitor. I simply turned up the brightness to make the display visible again. (I also turned on Windows 95's automatic **screen saver.**)

Get professional help

OK. If you've made sure the power is on and made sure that the monitor settings—such as the brightness and contrast—are not set to some wacky value, it may be that your monitor is broken. A monitor repairperson tells me, by the way, that if a monitor is ready to fail, it usually does so when you turn it on.

WINDOWS AND APPLICATIONS

You Can't Get an Application to Respond

It's unlikely but still possible that a **bug** in an **application** will cause the application to stop responding or, in computer parlance, to "hang." If this happens, you won't be able to choose menu commands in that application. (You will still be able to choose menu commands in other applications, though.) And you might not be able to move the mouse pointer or click the **mouse.** (In my experience, the mouse pointer under these circumstances usually looks like an hourglass or disappears completely.)

Try patience

It's possible that the application isn't actually unresponsive. It's possible that it's busy working on something you told it to do. Like saving the **document** on a **disk.** It's even possible that the application is busy working on something you didn't tell it to do. A word processor application might be busy breaking a long document into pages, for example.

For this reason, the first thing I'd try is a short break. Perhaps coffee and a cinnamon roll. I'm sure, too, that this strategy, which I've adopted as my own first defense, has nothing to do with my growing weight problem. It couldn't.

Terminate the hung application

Unfortunately, if an application truly is unresponsive— if it ignores your keyboard and mouse actions—there's nothing you can do to make it start responding again. When this happens, however, you can press Ctrl+Alt+Del. (You'll have to find these 3 keys on your keyboard first, of course.)

Pressing Ctrl+Alt+Del—you press the 3 keys simultaneously—tells **Windows 95** to look at each of the applications you've started, check for responsiveness, and display the Close Application **dialog box.**

continues

You Can't Get an Application to Respond *(continued)*

In the Close Application dialog box, Windows 95 identifies any unresponsive application as "not responding." To terminate an application, including one that is hung, select it, and then click the End command button. To remove the Close Application dialog box, click the Close button.

You Get an Application Error

Sometimes an **application** asks **Windows 95** to do the impossible. When this happens, Windows 95 displays a message box that says there's been an accident and that you had better come quickly.

Close the application

When Windows 95 alerts you to an application error, it usually gives you 2 choices: Close and Details. You want to choose Close. Details just gives you the gory specifics of what caused the application to go toes up.

It's also possible in rare cases for Windows 95 to give you the option of ignoring the error. Even in this case, however, the most prudent choice is still to close the application.

By the way, if you've been working with a **document** and have made changes you haven't yet saved, and you have the option of ignoring the error, you should ignore the application error and then save the document. Do save the document using a new file name, however. You don't want to replace the previous version of a document with a new corrupted document. Then once you've saved the document, close the application.

PRINTING

Your Printer Won't Print

A printer that won't print is usually easy to fix. Really. There are only a handful of things that might be wrong.

Verify that the printer is on

Sounds silly, doesn't it? But go ahead and check this first.

Verify that the printer is cabled correctly

A printer **cable** connects your computer and printer. This is the conduit that your computer uses to send information to your printer. Make sure that this cable is plugged firmly into both the computer and the printer. While you're at it, make sure that all of the other cables are also plugged firmly into their sockets.

And, oh yes. There's often more than 1 socket plug, or **port,** on the back of your computer into which a printer cable plugs. So you'll also want to make sure that you're plugging the printer cable into the correct port. Usually your printer cable plugs into the LPT1 port. (The port might even be labeled as "LPT1.")

Verify that the printer is on line

There should be an "Online" light somewhere on the front of your printer, indicating that your printer is ready and willing to accept information from your computer. This light should be on. If it isn't, put the printer on line. You usually do this by pressing an Online button or the reset button. If you can't find either of these buttons on your printer, take a peek at the user guide that came with your printer.

Add the printer if you haven't already

In **Windows 95,** you need to add a new printer before you can use it. To add a new printer, you use a wizard. Thank goodness this is the case, too, because the wizard makes everything really easy. All you have to do is open the Printers folder (such as by using **Windows Explorer**) and then double-click the Add Printer **icon.** Windows 95 starts the Add Printer Wizard and steps you through the process of describing your new printer. Don't worry; Windows 95 does most of the work for you. If you can read the manufacturer's name and the model name from the front of the printer, you're set.

continues

Your Printer Won't Print *(continued)*

Is your printer broken?

If none of the solutions described here work, it's possible that your printer is broken. In this case, there's nothing you can do from inside Windows 95. If you've tried everything and nothing has helped, try to print a test page. You might also want to follow any troubleshooting directions described in the printer's user guide. By trying these approaches, you'll be able to determine whether the printer is, in fact, broken. If your printer is broken, you'll need to take it to someone who re-pairs printers.

 Printers

You Want to Cancel a Printing Document

If you've told an **application** to print a **document** that you later realize you don't need or want, you might want to cancel the print job, particularly if the document is long or your printer is slow.

Cancel printing from within the application

If an application displays a message on the screen that says it's printing a document, you might be able to cancel the printing from within the application.

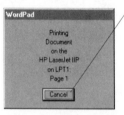

You can cancel the printing of this document just by clicking Cancel.

Cancel printing using Windows 95

When an application prints a document, what it really does is create a printable copy of the document and send this copy to **Windows 95.** Windows 95 then prints this printable copy—called a "spool file"—as well as any printable copies of documents that other applica-tions have sent it. (Remember that you might be running more than 1 application, so it's possible that more than 1 application is sending spool files to Windows 95.)

To cancel printing using Windows 95, open the Printers **folder** by clicking Start, choosing Settings and Printers, and then double-clicking the **icon** for the printer to which you've been sending the spool files. Windows 95 displays a print queue for the printer.

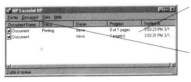

1 Select the printing document you want to cancel.

2 Choose the Document Cancel Printing command.

You Want to Postpone Printing a Document

If you've got a long **document** that you want to print eventually—but not quite yet—you can tell **Windows 95** to cool its heels for that particular spool file.

Pause the printing of the document

To pause the printing of a particular document, open the Printers **folder** by double-clicking it, and then double-click the **icon** for the printer to which you've been sending the spool files. Windows 95 then displays a print queue for the printer.

1 Select the printing document you want to pause.

2 Choose the Document Pause Printing command.

When you want to print the document later, repeat this process. Choosing the Document Pause Printing command a second time will resume the printing.

Your Printer Stalls

Some documents—such as those that combine color and graphics—are very slow to print. This slowness, besides causing you irritation, can cause your printer problems. **Windows 95** expects to be able to send your printer more data regularly (often every 45 seconds). If it takes 3 minutes to print a page, however, Windows 95 can't send the printer more data and might conclude that your printer isn't responding. Shortly after reaching this conclusion, Windows 95 will stop sending stuff to the printer. It may also display an on-screen message that reads something like, "That printer of yours isn't responding again, and I'm pretty much at my wits' end."

Tell Windows 95 to retry

To tell Windows 95 to start printing again, display the printer folder window, and choose the Printer Pause Printing command. (To display the printer folder window, click Start and then choose Settings and Printers.) Then open the stalled printer by double-clicking its **icon.** Or if Windows 95 displays a message box telling you that your darn printer has stalled, you can choose the Retry command button if it appears in the message box. This might be all you need to do. If several pages still remain to be printed in your presentation, you might need to sit in front of your computer and choose either the Printer Pause Printing command or the Retry button a few more times.

Increase the printer's Transmission Retry setting

If you're getting the "Printer isn't responding" message frequently or if you're going to be printing a lot of presentations, you might want to tell Windows 95 that it's OK that your printer isn't quite as quick as Windows 95 would like it to be. To do this, take the following steps:

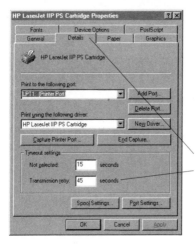

1 Open the Printers folder by clicking Start and the choosing Settings and Printers.

2 Open the printer that's stalling by double-clicking it.

3 Choose the Printer Properties command.

4 Click the Details **tab.**

5 Set the Transmission Retry value to something big. Something really big.

Setting the Transmission Retry value

The Transmission Retry value, in essence, tells Windows 95 how long to wait for a printer before notifying you that the printer isn't responding. For non-PostScript printers, Windows 95 assumes 45 seconds is long enough. For PostScript printers, Windows 95 assumes 90 seconds is long enough. But if you're printing graphics or you're printing in color, you can and should dramatically increase these settings. And I do mean dramatically. The suggested setting for a color PostScript printer, for example, is 900. Ugh.

FILES

You Want to Move a File to a Computer That's Running MS-DOS or an Earlier Version of Windows

Even though you've made the big switch to Windows 95, you'll have friends who haven't. You know who I'm talking about, right? It'll probably be the same people who still have platform shoes and lava lamps. So what happens when you want to use one of their **files** or when they want to use one of yours?

Use the network

If these friends are on your **network**—which is possible, I guess, although doubtful—you can share your files by saving them on a network disk drive and opening them from that drive. You can use **Windows Explorer** to do your saving and opening. Your friends can use File Manager.

Use a floppy disk

You can use **floppy disks** to move Windows 95 files to and from a computer that's running **MS-DOS.** This works because Windows 95 actually uses 2 names for every file: a long file name that you use in Windows 95 and in any Windows 95 applications and a short file name that MS-DOS and MS-DOS applications happily use.

The special new version of MS-DOS included with Windows 95 lets you display a directory list of file names that includes both the short, 8-character file name and the long file name. To do this, start MS-DOS (such as by clicking the **Start button** and then choosing Programs and MS-DOS).

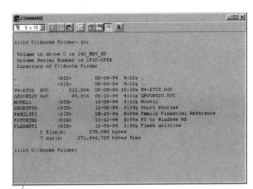

Type the command name *dir* to see the short and long file names of the files in a directory.

You Can't Save a File on Any Disk

Applications need a certain amount of system resources to save **files.** If these system resources get too low, you can run into some pretty serious problems. Fortunately, as long as you keep your cool, this doesn't have to be a disaster. Your basic tack is a simple one. You want to free up your system resources and then try resaving the file, or **document.**

Close any other applications

Switch to any of the other open applications, and close them. You can switch to an open application by clicking its button on the **Taskbar.** Then choose from several ways to close the application. Probably the easiest way is to click the application window's Close button.

Close any documents you don't need to save

If you've opened other documents in the application, you might be able to free up system resources by closing those other documents. Of course, this might present its own problem if the other documents also need to be saved. In extreme cases, you might need to close the document that has the fewest unsaved changes without saving it.

You Can't Save or Copy a File to a Floppy Disk

If you try to save a file or copy a file to a **floppy disk** but can't, you can try several approaches.

Unprotect the floppy disk

If you get a message that says a disk is write-protected, you won't be able to save a file on, or "write to," the disk until you unprotect the disk.

To write to a 5¼-inch floppy disk, verify that the floppy disk has a notch. If a piece of tape or an adhesive tab is covering this notch, you won't be able to write anything to the disk. To unprotect the floppy disk, remove the tape or adhesive tab that covers the notch.

To write to a 3½-inch floppy disk, verify that there is no square hole in the disk's upper right corner when you're holding the disk so that you can read its label. If there is a square hole, flip the floppy disk over, and move the slide so that it covers the hole.

Why the write-protection?

I don't mean to sound like a worrier, but before you decide it's OK to write to a previously write-protected floppy disk, you may want to consider the reasons someone protected the disk. Who knows? Maybe there's stuff on the disk that shouldn't be written over.

Format the floppy disk if needed

If you get a message that a Windows-based application can't read a disk, it may be because the disk isn't formatted. If you know this is the case or if you know there's nothing on the floppy disk that you or anyone else needs, you can format the floppy disk. (For all practical purposes, formatting a disk destroys everything that's on it.) I should also tell you that if you get a message that a Windows-based application can't read a disk, it may be because the disk is bad. In this case, rather than format the floppy, you should probably just throw the thing away.

164

You Can't Find a File

I love large **hard disks**. It's great, just great, to have hundreds and hundreds of **megabytes** (**MB**) of storage. All that room makes it easy to misplace a **file,** however. Fortunately, **Windows 95** provides an extremely powerful tool for finding lost files: the Find File **application.**

Because the Find File application is so powerful and so terribly useful, I'm going to describe it in detail here.

Use the Find File application

To start the Find File application, click the **Start button.** Next choose Find and then Files Or Folders. Windows 95 displays the Find: All Files dialog box.

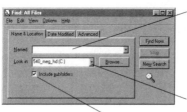

1 If you know the file name, type it in the Named box. You can use **wildcard characters** as part of the file name.

2 Use the Look In **drop-down list box** to tell Windows 95 on which disk to look.

3 Click the Include Subfolders check box if you want to look in both the **folders** and **subfolders** of the disk you identified using the Look In box.

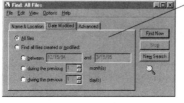

4 Optionally, use the options in the Date Modified **tab** to describe the last modification date of the file you're looking for.

continues

You Can't Find a File *(continued)*

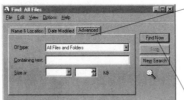

5 Optionally, use the options in the Advanced tab to describe either some string of text that a file contains or the file size.

6 Click Find Now to start the search for the file or files you've described. When Windows 95 completes its search, it displays a list of any files it has found in the Find: All Files window.

Multitasking is cool

If you describe a sophisticated search—say, one that looks for chunks of text in files—the search can take a long time. Perhaps hours or even days. But this doesn't have to be a problem. You can run other applications at the same time. All you need to do is start the other applications.

 Multitasking; Starting Windows-Based Applications

You Can't Open a File

If you can find a **file** but you can't open it, you've got another problem. There are several reasons why you might not be able to open a file. Most of the reasons, however, are easy to address.

Verify that the file isn't already open

It's possible that another **application** has already opened the file. If that's the case, you won't be able to open the same file a second time. So you'll need to first close the file using the application that's currently got it open. Or if you can't close the file until another application finishes whatever it's doing, you'll just have to wait.

Use an application instead of Windows Explorer

If you tell **Windows Explorer** to open a document, it first opens the application that created the document and then tells that application to open the document. But there's a potential problem. When Windows Explorer names the document that should be opened, it uses the long-style file name acceptable to Windows 95. If you're using an MS-DOS application or an application designed for an earlier version of Windows, however, this application will get all wigged out because it expects a file name of no more than 8 characters. It'll finally give up, telling you that it can't open a file that has a name like the one you've supplied.

Fortunately, there's an easy solution to this problem. Just use the application that created the document to open the document. You open the document in the usual way.

Your Hard Disk Is Full

If your **hard disk** begins to fill up, you'll either want to free up some space or buy a bigger disk—for two reasons. First, **Windows 95** likes a certain amount of free disk space just to run because it uses **virtual memory.** Second, some Windows-based applications go, like, totally berserk if they encounter a full hard disk. (By "totally berserk," I just mean you'll get an application error.)

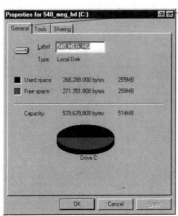

Check your free disk space by starting **Windows Explorer,** clicking the hard disk's **icon,** and then choosing the File Properties command. The General **tab** in the Properties dialog box includes a pie chart that shows free disk space.

continues

Your Hard Disk is Full *(continued)*

Erase any unneeded files

The most direct way to free up disk space is to remove individual **files** from the disk using Windows Explorer's File Delete command. If you want to save the files, you can first copy them to a **floppy disk.**

In general, it's not a good idea to remove files you didn't create in the first place. It may be, for example, that you and Windows 95 or you and some **application** have different ideas about whether a file is needed.

Empty the Recycle Bin, and reduce its size

The Recycle Bin, as you may know, stores deleted files. Windows 95 allocates a set percentage of your disk space—the default percentage is 10%—for storing the Recycle Bin's files.

The Recycle Bin is cool, no doubt. But it does use a lot of disk space. So one way to recover some disk space is to either empty the Recycle Bin or at least delete some of its files. Then after either of these actions, you can reduce the Recycle Bin's size. To reduce its size, follow these steps:

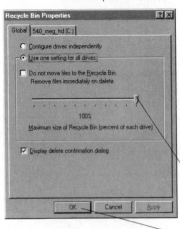

1 Display the Recycle Bin window (such as by double-clicking the Recycle Bin or by opening the Recycle Bin icon using Windows Explorer).

2 Choose the File Empty Recycle Bin command.

3 Choose the File Properties command.

4 Move the slide control to the left so that the Recycle Bin reserves less space.

5 Click OK.

You Accidentally Erased a File

If you erase, or delete, a **file** and later realize you shouldn't have, there's a very good chance you'll be able to recover it. As you might know, the Recycle Bin stores deleted files. So any recently deleted file is probably still stored in the Recycle Bin. (Note that when the Recycle Bin eventually does fill up, **Windows 95** makes room for newly deleted files in the Recycle Bin by removing the oldest deleted files from it. So you won't be able to undelete really old files using the Recycle Bin.)

Undelete the file in the Recycle Bin

To undelete a file you've previously deleted—but that still appears in the Recycle Bin, follow these steps:

1 Display the Recycle Bin window (such as by double-clicking the Recycle Bin icon or by opening the Recycle Bin using **Windows Explorer**).

2 Select the file you want to undelete.

3 Choose the File Restore command.

Undelete the file using another approach

If you can't find a file in the Recycle Bin, all is not lost. When Windows 95 deletes a file from the Recycle Bin, it doesn't actually remove the file from your **hard disk.** Instead, it just crosses the file off of its list of "files to keep track of" and stops protecting the disk space used to store that file. Eventually, the lack of protection means that the file's disk space will be overwritten with another, new file. But until that happens, you can usually recover the file.

To undelete one of these files, you can use either of 2 approaches. You can use the old MS-DOS delete application, which should still appear in the DOS directory of your PC if you upgraded to Windows 95. Or you can use one of the delete applications available from third-party software application providers. Because the precise steps for undeleting a file depend on the particular delete tool, your best tactic is to follow the instructions that describe the delete application you want to use.

continues

You Accidentally Erased a File *(continued)*

Let me say one other thing. Unless you're using a delete application that's written specifically to be used with Windows 95, you need to be really careful about how you undelete files. There's some chance, for example, that you'll foul up, or corrupt, Windows 95's long file names if you undelete files using the old MS-DOS delete application. (It's probably a good idea to back up your hard disk before you try undeleting files.)

In general, I'm sort of a scaredy-cat anyway, but I would also suggest that you not undelete files using an old delete application unless the files are very, very important—so valuable, in fact, that it's worth risking corrupting a bunch of stuff that's already on your hard disk. If you do corrupt application files and data files that are already stored on your hard disk, you'll need to restore the data files from a backup copy of the files (if the backup copy is available) and reinstall the applications.

QUICK REFERENCE

Need help you haven't been able to get in the preceding pages? Don't worry. Or at least not yet. The "Quick Reference" section provides a list of technical support telephone numbers for just about every hardware manufacturer and software developer.

MY PERSONAL COMPUTER DESCRIPTION:

Microprocessor: _____

Memory: _____ x _____

Monitor: _____

Video card: _____

Sound card: _____

Hard disk drive: _____

Floppy disk drive: _____

Modem: _____

CD-ROM drive: _____

Other devices: _____

_____

_____

_____

HARDWARE MANUFACTURERS' TECHNICAL SUPPORT AND CUSTOMER NUMBERS

Company	Technical support phone	Sales and service phone
Acer America Corporation	1-800-445-6495	1-800-368-2237
ACMA Computers, Inc.	1-800-786-8998	1-800-786-6888
Apple Computer, Inc.	1-800-767-2775	1-800-538-9696
AST Research, Inc.	1-800-727-1278	1-800-876-4278
Austin Direct/IPC Corporation	1-800-752-4171	1-800-752-1577
Blackship Computer Systems, Inc.	1-800-531-7447	1-800-531-7447
Brother Industries, Ltd.	1-800-276-7746	1-800-276-7746
BSI Broadax Systems, Inc.	1-818-442-7038	1-800-872-4547

Company	Technical support phone	Sales and service phone
Canon USA, Inc.	1-800-423-2366	1-800-848-4123
Citizen America	1-310-453-0614	1-800-477-4683
Compaq Computer Corporation	1-800-652-6672	1-800-345-1518
CTX International, Inc.	1-800-888-2017 (Notebooks) 1-800-888-2012 (Monitors)	1-909-595-6146
Dell Computer Corporation	1-800-624-9896	1-800-274-3355
Diamond Flower Electric Instrument Co. (USA), Inc.	1-916-568-1234	1-800-275-3342
Digital Equipment Corporation	1-800-777-4343 (Printers and terminals) 1-800-344-4825 (General tech. consulting)	1-800-344-4825
Epson America, Inc.	1-800-922-8911	1-800-289-3776
Ergo Computing, Inc.	1-800-633-1922	1-800-633-1925
Fujitsu Computer Products of America	1-408-894-3950	1-800-626-4686
Gateway 2000, Inc.	1-800-846-2301	1-800-846-2042
GCC Technologies, Inc.	1-617-276-8620	1-800-422-7777
Hewlett-Packard Company	1-208-323-2551	1-800-752-0900
IBM Corporation	1-800-772-2227	1-800-426-2255
Intel Corporation	1-800-628-8686	1-800-628-8686
Intelesys, Inc.	1-800-873-5551	1-510-326-6300 (ext. 165)
Lasermaster Technologies	1-612-944-9331	1-800-365-4646
Lexmark International, Inc.	1-800-358-5838	1-800-358-5838
Mannesmann Tally Corporation	1-800-251-5593	1-800-843-1347
Micron Computer	1-800-223-6571	1-800-223-6571
Midwest Micro	1-800-204-0583	1-800-572-8844
MIS (Microniche Information Systems, Inc.)	1-800-733-9188	1-800-733-9188
NEC Corporation	1-800-388-8888	1-800-632-4636
Netis Technology, Inc.	1-800-577-7526	1-800-577-7526
Okidata, Division of Oki America, Inc.	1-609-273-0300	1-800-654-3282
Panasonic Communications and Systems Company (a subsidiary of Matsushita Electric Corporation of America)	1-800-742-8086	1-800-742-8086

continues

Hardware Manufacturers' Technical Support and Customer Numbers
(continued)

Company	Technical support phone	Sales and service phone
Polywell Computers	1-800-999-1278	1-800-999-1278
Quantex Microsystems, Inc.	1-800-864-8650	1-800-288-0566
Robotech, Inc.	1-801-565-0645	1-800-533-0633
Tagram System Corporation	1-800-443-5761	1-800-824-7267
Texas Instruments, Inc.	1-800-848-3927	1-800-848-3927
Toshiba America Information Systems, Inc.	1-800-999-4273	1-800-334-3445
USA Flex, Inc.	1-800-USA-FLEX	1-800-USA-FLEX
VTech Industries	1-800-967-3976	1-800-215-3976
WinBook Computer Corporation	1-800-468-1225	1-800-468-7502
Xerox Corporation	1-800-822-2979	1-800-275-9376
ZDS Zenith Data Systems, Inc.	1-800-227-3360	1-800-533-0331
Zeos International	1-800-423-5891	1-800-423-5891
Other		

SOFTWARE DEVELOPERS' TECHNICAL SUPPORT AND CUSTOMER NUMBERS

Company	Technical support phone	Sales and service phone
Adobe Systems, Inc. (Aldus Corporation)	1-800-628-2320 (Aldus/Pre-Adobe products) 1-800-642-3623 (Adobe products)	1-800-628-2320
AT&T	1-800-531-2222	1-800-637-2600
Borland International, Inc.	1-408-461-9000	1-800-331-0877
Broderbund Software, Inc.	1-415-382-4700	1-800-521-6263
Compton's NewMedia, Inc.	1-800-893-5458	(Sold only through retail outlets)
Creative Labs, Inc.	1-405-742-6622	1-408-428-6600
DataStorm Technologies, Inc.	1-314-875-0530	1-314-443-3282
DeLorme Mapping	1-207-865-7098	1-800-452-5931

Company	Technical support phone	Sales and service phone
Delrina Corporation	1-416-444-4628 (Consumer Software Division for screen savers, calendars, etc.)	
1-416-443-4390 (Winfax Pro, etc.)	1-800-268-6082	
IBM Corporation	1-800-772-2227	1-800-426-2255
Intuit, Inc.	1-800-624-8742	1-800-624-8742
Lotus Development Corporation	1-800-386-8600 (Windows) 1-404-399-5505 (Word processing)	1-800-223-1662 (DOS/OS2/Mac Desktop) 1-800-343-5414
Microsoft Corporation	1-206-454-2030	1-800-426-9400
Novell, Inc.	1-800-NET-WARE 1-801-429-7000 (All other software)	1-800-NET-WARE (Pre-sales) 1-800-346-7177 (Add-ons or other sales)
Origin Systems, Inc.	1-512-335-0440	1-800-245-4525
Peachtree Software (A subsidiary of Automatic Data Processing, Inc.)	1-404-564-5700	1-800-247-3224
QuarterDeck Office Systems, Inc.	1-310-392-9701	1-800-354-3260
Saber Software Corporation	1-800-526-8086	1-800-338-8754
Sierra On-Line, Inc.	1-206-644-4343	1-800-757-7707
Software Publishing Corporation	1-408-986-8000	1-408-986-8000
The Learning Company	1-510-796-3030	1-800-852-2255
Other		

E

F

The manuscript for this book was prepared and submitted to Microsoft Press in electronic form. Text files were prepared using Microsoft Word 6.0 for Windows. Pages were composed by Stephen L. Nelson, Inc., using PageMaker 5.0 for Windows, with text in Minion and display type in Copperplate. Composed pages were delivered to the printer as electronic prepress files.

COVER DESIGNER
Rebecca Geisler-Johnson

COVER ILLUSTRATOR
Eldon Doty

INTERIOR TEXT DESIGNER
The Understanding Business

ENVIRONMENT ILLUSTRATIONS
Stefan Knorr

PAGE LAYOUT, TYPOGRAPHY
Stefan Knorr

COPY EDITOR
Barbara Browne

TECHNICAL EDITOR
Beth Shannon and Jack Valko

INDEXER
Julie Kawabata

WRITERS
Peter Weverka and Steve Nelson

Printed on recycled paper stock.